EYEWITNESS
ARCTIC &
ANTARCTIC

Alpine azalea

Net for catching ptarmigan

Nenets child's winter parka

Antarctic explorer's compass

Red star fish

Model of a Nenets tent

Adélie penguin

Northern
fleabane

Antarctic
krill

EYEWITNESS
ARCTIC &
ANTARCTIC

Written by
BARBARA TAYLOR

Photographed by
GEOFF BRIGHTLING

Carving of a
polar bear
from Canada

Walrus

Ammonite fossil

Polar bear

Model of a Greenland kayak

DK | Penguin Random House

REVISED EDITION

DK DELHI
Senior Editor Neha Ruth Samuel
Senior Art Editor Vikas Chauhan
Art Editor Tanvi Sahu
Assistant Art Editor Prateek Maurya
Senior Picture Researcher Sumedha Chopra
Managing Editor Kingshuk Ghoshal
Managing Art Editor Govind Mittal
DTP Designers Deepak Mittal, Nityanand Kumar
Production Editor Pawan Kumar
Jacket Designer Vidushi Chaudhry
Senior Jackets Coordinator Priyanka Sharma Saddi

DK LONDON
Senior Editor Georgina Palffy
Project Art Editor Kit Lane
Senior US Editor Megan Douglass
US Executive Editor Lori Cates Hand
Managing Editor Francesca Baines
Managing Art Editor Philip Letsu
Production Controller Jack Matts
Jackets Design Development Manager Sophia MTT
Publisher Andrew Macintyre
Associate Publishing Director Liz Wheeler
Art Director Karen Self
Publishing Director Jonathan Metcalf

Consultants Dr. Simon Morley,
Dr. Elizabeth Ann Walsh, Dr. Pearl Brower

FIRST EDITION
Project Editor Gillian Denton
Art Editor Jane Tetzlaff
Managing Editor Simon Adams
Managing Art Editor Julia Harris
Researcher Céline Carez
Editorial Assistance Djinn von Noorden, David Pickering
Production Catherine Semark
Picture Research Clive Webster

This Eyewitness ® Guide has been conceived by
Dorling Kindersley Limited and Editions Gallimard

This American Edition, 2024
First American Edition, 1995
Published in the United States by DK Publishing,
a division of Penguin Random House LLC
1745 Broadway, 20th Floor, New York, NY 10019

A catalog record for this book is available from the Library of Congress.
ISBN 978-0-5938-4242-3 (Paperback)
ISBN 978-0-5938-4243-0 (ALB)

DK books are available at special discounts when purchased in bulk
for sales promotions, premiums, fund-raising, or educational use.
For details, contact: DK Publishing Special Markets,
1745 Broadway, 20th Floor, New York, NY 10019
SpecialSales@dk.com

Printed and bound in China

www.dk.com

Game board made from walrus tusk

Sámi boots

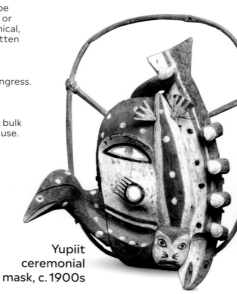
Antarctic lichen

Yupiit ceremonial mask, c. 1900s

Contents

Snowy owl

The ends of the Earth

The two polar regions are among the coldest places on the planet. A huge, frozen ocean—the Arctic—surrounds the North Pole, while a vast area of frozen land—Antarctica—surrounds the South Pole. Although they are at opposite ends of the planet, they have many things in common, such as long, dark winters and short, light summers.

The Arctic

Antarctica

The positions of the Arctic and Antarctica

Trapped by the ice
In 1596, the ship of the Dutch cartographer Willem Barentsz was trapped by Arctic sea ice for almost a year. Barentsz and his crew built a lodge from the wrecked ship to survive.

A white world
Ice dominates the landscapes and seascapes of the polar regions. The Antarctic Peninsula is accessible to tourist ships in summer, when the sea ice has broken up into small fragments. Once winter comes, the water will completely freeze over again.

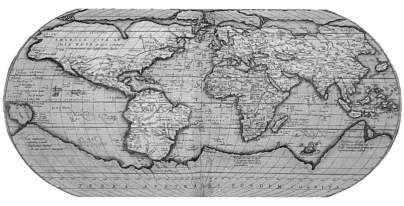

The unknown land

While Polynesian voyagers may have reached Antarctica by the 7th century, Europeans knew very little about the region until James Cook's journeys in the 18th century. Ancient European maps named the region *Terra Australis Incognita* (Latin for "the unknown southern continent").

The auroras

Known as the northern and southern lights, auroras are wispy curtains of light that appear in the sky over the lower polar regions. They are formed when charged particles from the sun strike gases in Earth's atmosphere, making the gases give off light.

Midnight sun

In regions near the poles, the sun never sets during summer and never rises in winter. This is because of Earth's tilt toward the sun. While one pole has constant daylight, the other is shrouded in darkness.

Ice built up from centuries of snowfalls flows slowly downhill and extends over the sea as an ice shelf.

This vast iceberg may be tens or hundreds of yards thick.

Sea ice is usually less than 16 ft (5 m) thick and may be continuous or fragmented.

The Arctic and **tundra**

At the center of the Arctic region is a vast area of permanently frozen ice floating on the Arctic Ocean. The Arctic also includes the world's largest island, Greenland, and the northern edges of North America, Asia, and Europe. South of the Arctic ice is the tundra, which means "treeless plain" in Russian. This low, flat landscape is home to lichens, mosses, grasses, low bushes, and tiny trees.

Permafrost

A permanently frozen layer called permafrost occurs below the surface of the Arctic soil. The ground above the permafrost thaws in summer and the water collects on the surface, forming lakes and marshes. Buildings and roads have to be specially insulated to avoid melting the permafrost, or they begin to collapse.

Marshy pools form because permafrost prevents water from draining away.

Only low-growing plants can survive the intense cold and fierce winter winds of the tundra.

Bears

Polar bears live only in the Arctic. They make long journeys across the sea ice, hunting for seals. The bears are expert divers and swimmers, and often hitch rides on ice floes.

Frozen layer, called permafrost, lies a little way below the surface.

At the edge of the ocean, ice forms in winter and melts again in summer.

The **thickness** of the **permafrost** can be up to **3,000 ft (900 m)**.

Permanent sea ice lasts from year to year.

Moving sea ice that melts and breaks up in summer and refreezes in winter is called pack ice.

Ice floes are drifting fragments of sea ice.

Alpine azalea (Kalmia procumbens), a member of the heather family, grows across the Arctic region.

Sinking the unsinkable

Icebergs are huge chunks of floating ice that originate from land glaciers and ice shelves. The supposedly unsinkable ship *Titanic* sank in April 1912 after hitting an iceberg. The *Titanic*'s iceberg, like others encountered in the North Atlantic, originated in Greenland.

Summer in Denali National Park, Alaska

Plants

Arctic plants have adapted in various ways to the low temperatures and short growing season of the region. They grow rapidly in spring to take advantage of long periods of daylight. There are more than 500 species of wild flower, and in summer, the Arctic is ablaze with color.

Antarctica

The continent of Antarctica is twice the size of Australia and three times higher than any other continent—almost all of it is covered by an ice sheet that is, on average, 7,087 ft (2,160 m) thick. This height is a major reason for the extreme cold—the average winter temperature for the interior of the continent is –76°F (–60°C). Antarctica's severe climate and its isolation limit the variety of its wildlife. The largest animal living on land all year round is an insect, but other animals flock to Antarctica in summer to breed and feed.

Hardy survivors
Lichens, such as this (*Usnea aurantiaco-atra*), as well as liverworts and mosses, are among the few plants able to grow on land in Antarctica.

Warmer past
Antarctica was not always cold. Fossil ferns provide evidence of a warmer, subtropical climate about 70 million years ago (mya).

Penguins
These flightless birds are fast swimmers. They live only in the southern hemisphere. Most species, including Adélie penguins (*Pygoscelis adeliae*) seen here, nest on snow-free pockets of land in summer, when the sea teems with fish. Emperor penguins, on the other hand, breed in the harsh Antarctic winter.

Coiled clues
Ammonites—shelled mollusks with coiled shells—swam in subtropical waters until they died out 66 mya. Fossil ammonites found in Antarctica show that its seas were warmer millions of years ago.

Spiral shell

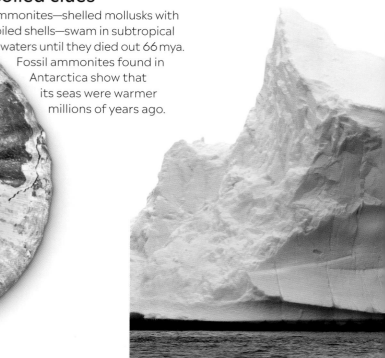

WEIGHT OF ICE

About 98 percent of Antarctica is covered by a vast ice sheet, which in some places is more than 2½ miles (4 km) thick. Only a few mountain peaks stick out. The weight of the ice pushes most of the rocky surface below sea level. The ice at the bottom of the ice sheet may be at least 2.7 million years old.

2.7-million-year-old ice

+1.8 miles (3 km)

+1.2 miles (2 km)

+0.6 miles (1 km)

Sea level

-0.6 miles (1 km)

Dry valleys

In the middle of the continent, among the Transantarctic Mountains, are vast dry valleys not covered by snow or ice all year round. Winds rush down the valleys, sucking away any moisture from the rock. Antarctica gets so little rainfall or precipitation that it is classified as a desert—in fact, the largest in the world.

Icebreakers

Ships called icebreakers clear routes through frozen polar seas. With a specially shaped bow and a reinforced hull, they push the bow on top of the ice until the weight of the ship breaks through.

Colossal icebergs

Snowfall on Antarctica turns into ice, which compacts and flows down toward the coastal ice shelves. Ocean currents and waves break up the ice shelves, creating icebergs. Some icebergs are up to 186 miles (300 km) long and 25 miles (40 km) wide. Large icebergs can be tracked by satellites for years before they melt.

As icebergs melt, they often form fascinating shapes.

The ice is eroded and carved by sea water and wind.

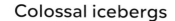

In Antarctic waters

There is a greater variety of life in the Antarctic Ocean than in the Arctic Ocean. In shallow waters, ice scrapes against the seabed, limiting the kinds of organism that can live there, but in deeper waters below most of the ice, there is an incredible wealth of life. This includes corals, anemones, and about 300 varieties of sponges. The cold affects the life cycle of many inhabitants. In the cold, animals function slowly and produce fewer, larger eggs. Many of these animals live longer than their counterparts in warmer climates.

Tube feet

Star turn
Starfish (*Asterias rubens*) locate their prey by smell and grasp it using the rows of suckered tube feet on their arms. The seabed around Antarctica is sometimes covered with red starfish (*Odontaster validus*).

Spiny legs are raised up to appear larger in front of predators.

Cold giants
Among the Antarctic's bottom-living invertebrates (creatures without backbones) is this giant Antarctic isopod (*Glyptonotus antarcticus*). It grows up to 8 in (20 cm), about three times bigger than similar species elsewhere. *Glyptonotus* eats anything and scavenges around the seabed.

Dual-purpose spines
The Antarctic sea urchin (*Sterechinus neumayeri*) uses its dense covering of mobile spines for both movement and defense.

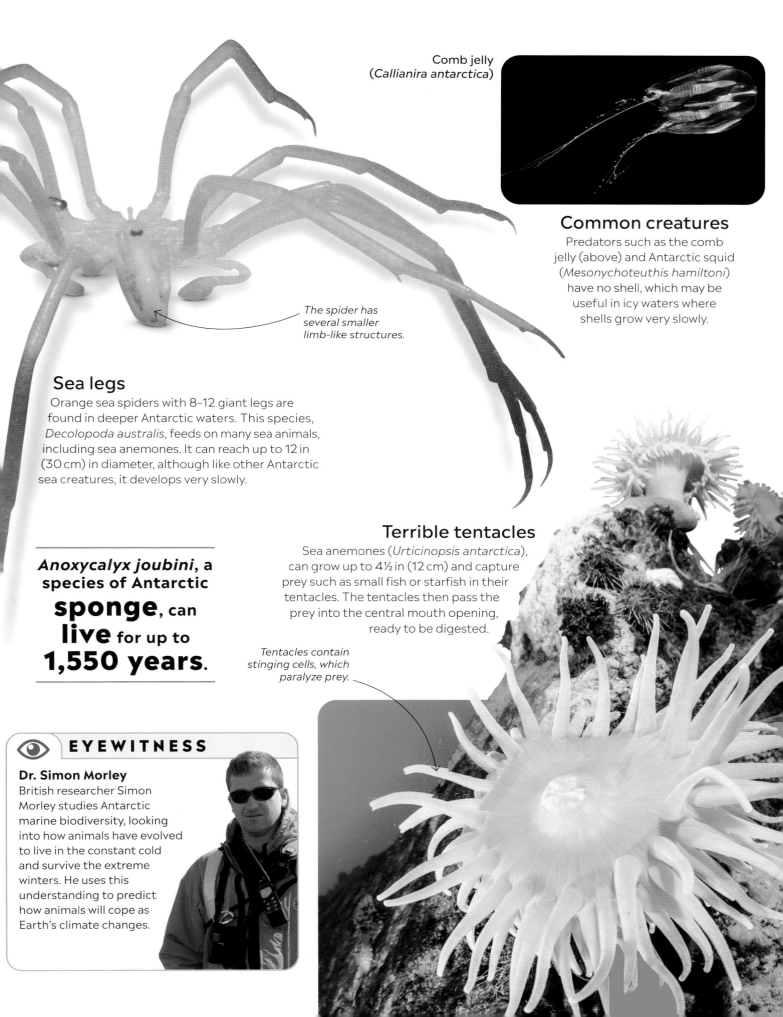

Comb jelly
(*Callianira antarctica*)

Common creatures

Predators such as the comb jelly (above) and Antarctic squid (*Mesonychoteuthis hamiltoni*) have no shell, which may be useful in icy waters where shells grow very slowly.

The spider has several smaller limb-like structures.

Sea legs

Orange sea spiders with 8–12 giant legs are found in deeper Antarctic waters. This species, *Decolopoda australis*, feeds on many sea animals, including sea anemones. It can reach up to 12 in (30 cm) in diameter, although like other Antarctic sea creatures, it develops very slowly.

Anoxycalyx joubini, a species of Antarctic **sponge**, can **live** for up to **1,550 years**.

Terrible tentacles

Sea anemones (*Urticinopsis antarctica*), can grow up to 4½ in (12 cm) and capture prey such as small fish or starfish in their tentacles. The tentacles then pass the prey into the central mouth opening, ready to be digested.

Tentacles contain stinging cells, which paralyze prey.

👁 EYEWITNESS

Dr. Simon Morley
British researcher Simon Morley studies Antarctic marine biodiversity, looking into how animals have evolved to live in the constant cold and survive the extreme winters. He uses this understanding to predict how animals will cope as Earth's climate changes.

Residents and **visitors**

The number and variety of animals living near the poles change dramatically with the seasons. Thousands of birds and mammals only visit the regions during the brief, light summer months, when it is relatively warm and food is plentiful. Here they can find safe places to rear their young, with few predators and little competition for food and nesting places.

Dense down feathers help keep the snow geese warm.

Long haul

The Arctic tern breeds in large colonies during the Arctic summer. It then flies all the way to Antarctica to take advantage of the almost constant daylight and rich food supply of the Antarctic summer.

Flight of the snow geese

Every summer, many thousands of snow geese migrate to the Arctic tundra to nest. They fly in flocks of tens of thousands from the Gulf of Mexico, covering a distance of about 2,000 miles (3,200 km).

Arctic tern
(Sterna paradisaea)

A thick skull and solid, horny band protect the brain when males clash horns.

Mighty musk ox

Tough, hardy musk oxen roam over the Arctic tundra in herds made up of females and young, led by one or more bulls. In summer, herds number about 10 animals, but in winter, musk oxen move south in herds of 50 or more, wherever they can find food under the snow.

Musk ox
(Ovibos moschatus)

The edges of musk ox hoofs are sharp enough to dig through thick snow and ice to reach mosses, lichens, and roots underneath.

Caribou
(*Rangifer tarandus*)

Summer holidays

Caribou are always on the move between their winter and summer feeding grounds. In spring, immense herds trek northward to feed on lichens and other low-growing tundra plants. As winter closes in, they move south once more to the shelter of the forests.

The birds save energy by flying in a V-formation in the slipstream of the one in front.

Snow goose
(*Anser caerulescens*)

Most migratory animals use the same routes for their journeys every year.

FOOD IN POLAR WATERS

Humpback whales of both the northern and southern hemispheres travel to cold polar waters in summer to take advantage of the rich food supply of plankton and fish. In winter, when the polar seas freeze over, they migrate back to warmer tropical waters to breed.

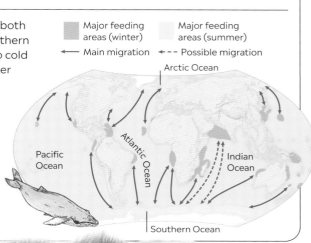

Major feeding areas (winter)
Major feeding areas (summer)
← Main migration
◄--- Possible migration

Arctic Ocean

Pacific Ocean

Atlantic Ocean

Indian Ocean

Southern Ocean

Dense woolly underfur and thick layers of fat under the skin keep the musk ox warm.

Adaptable animals

Polar animals that do not migrate have adapted to survive. Insects lay their eggs when the soil is warm, and the larvae can survive freezing winter temperatures. Some mammals grow thick winter fur, which is often white, to camouflage the animal against snow. Many mammals have a layer of fat under their skin for warmth and as a food store. Birds have layers of dense, fluffy feathers to keep out the cold. As summer arrives, birds and mammals molt their thick coats.

Antarctic ice fish
(*Chaenocephalus aceratus*)

Antifreeze in its veins

Many Antarctic fish have antifreeze chemicals in their bodies, enabling them to live in a "supercooled" state. This means their body fluids remain liquid at temperatures below the point at which ice forms.

Thick, bushy tail can be curled around the body for warmth during blizzards or when resting or sleeping.

Short legs lose less heat than long ones, because there is less surface area exposed to the air.

Arctic fox
(*Vulpes lagopus*)

Hair under the paws stops the fox sinking in snow.

Summer plumage

Rock ptarmigan (*Lagopus mutus*)

A bird for all seasons

Ptarmigans change their plumage twice a year to stay well camouflaged at all times. They also increase their feather density in winter, and sometimes burrow in snow when resting overnight to reduce heat loss.

Winter plumage

Functional fat

Whales, seals, and walruses are kept warm by a layer of thick fat called blubber. This walrus (*Odobenus rosmarus*) is in no danger of getting cold.

Small, round ears reduce heat loss.

Dressed for winter

The Arctic fox's white winter fur is made up of hollow hairs that are full of air. The air in the hairs traps body heat. Air is a good insulator and does not let heat pass through it easily. The Arctic fox can tolerate temperatures of –40°F (–40°C), or even lower.

Sharp claws to dig through the snow to find food

Dressed for summer

When summer arrives, the Arctic fox molts (sheds) its thick, white, winter coat and grows a thinner, brownish-gray coat, which matches the rocks of the tundra landscape. These colors make the fox hard to see, allowing it to hunt without being spotted. Arctic foxes have a varied diet ranging from berries, birds, and eggs to shells, dead animals, and garbage.

Pale maidens
(*Sisyrinchium filifolium*)

Flowers are both male and female.

Capsules contain seeds.

Survival of the fittest

Only specialized, hardy plants can survive the fierce winds, biting cold, thin soils, and short growing seasons of the polar lands. The most successful plants are the simple ones, such as mosses, lichens, and algae. In the short summer, flowers burst out and rapidly produce seeds before winter returns.

Long roots can obtain nitrogen and water even in harsh, dry conditions.

Pale maidens

This subantarctic iris has grasslike leaves. It is able to store food in fleshy roots underground. This ability helps it survive and grow quickly in spring.

Arctic wormwood (*Artemisia borealis*)

Flower heads are about ¼ in (5–6 mm) across.

Well anchored

The northern primrose (*Primula scandinavica*) produces many seeds in a capsule. This splits open and releases the seeds when they are ripe.

Most flowering plants in the Arctic grow low to the ground to avoid the winds.

Silky or hairless leaves are deeply divided.

Arctic wormwood

This hardy plant grows in colonies on dry, rocky ridges and gravel banks.

Flowers of Antarctica

The Antarctic pearlwort (*Colobanthus quitensis*) is one of the only two flowering plants found in the Antarctic region. It grows to about 2 in (5 cm) in height, and produces a mass of small, bright yellow flowers.

Great burnet

The great burnet (*Sanguisorba officinalis*) is widely spread in the northern hemisphere, and is also found in the Arctic. Its parts are used in traditional medicine to stop bleeding and to treat burns.

Woolly bear caterpillar of the tiger moth (*Arctia caja*)

Polar insect

Few pollinating insects can be found in polar lands. The Arctic regions are home to several types of butterfly and moth.

Insect repellent

Low, compact cushions of northern fleabane flower in the Arctic summer when the tundra lands become waterlogged with melted ice and snow. The plant is highly unattractive to fleas and midges, and can be used as an insect repellent.

Northern fleabane (*Erigeron borealis*)

Treeless tundra

The harsh climate; severe winds; and shallow, frozen soils of the Arctic tundra prevent most trees from growing. The small plants of the tundra grow slowly and are nearly all perennial (live longer than a year).

Growth of grass

Several hardy grasses grow well in polar lands. *Deschampsia cespitosa* thrives in the Arctic, while *Deschampsia antarctica*, commonly called Antarctic hair grass (left) is expanding across the Antarctic mainland due to rising temperatures. It is the region's only flowering plant apart from the Antarctic pearlwort.

Birds of the Arctic

Happy families

More than 100 million little auks (*Alle alle*) breed along Arctic coasts each summer. Little auks have a thick layer of fat under the skin to keep warm. They feed on small invertebrates and fish, storing food in a throat pouch.

On the tundra

Sandhill cranes (*Grus canadensis*) breed mostly in the tundra, laying their eggs on plants in undisturbed marshes. Young birds stay with their parents for nearly a year. These tall waders probe in the mud for worms and water creatures.

Most Arctic birds, such as waders, ducks, swans, and gulls, are migratory. Few birds endure the Arctic climate all year round, but residents include the ptarmigan, ivory gull, and little auk. The plumage of Arctic residents is denser than those of migratory birds, especially in winter, and their feet, protected by feathers, do not freeze to the ice. Many Arctic birds feed at sea, on fish and other marine animals. Most nest and rear their young on land in the summer.

Long neck helps bird probe in water beds.

ON DISPLAY

Cranes mate for life and perform spectacular courtship dances that involve moves such as head-bobbing, bowing, skipping, and leaping as high as 20 ft (6 m) in the air.

Streamlined, torpedo-shaped body for speed underwater.

Birds in art

Inuit artists often depict Arctic birds in their paintings and sculptures. Carvings, such as the toy shown below, may be made of stone, bone, or ivory, and are made and polished entirely by hand.

Moving the toy's two sticks back and forth causes the birds to bob down for food.

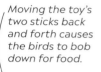

Slender, dagger-shaped beak snaps up fish and crustaceans.

Arctic loon

Loons, sometimes called divers, are adapted to swimming underwater. Their legs are set far back on the body, making them streamlined underwater but clumsy on land. Seen on the left is the black-throated loon (*Gavia arctica*), which breeds on tundra lakes and migrates mainly to the Pacific coast in winter.

Handsome breeding plumage; winter plumage is dull and grayish.

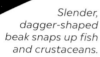

Feather beds

Eider ducks (*Somateria mollissima*) in the Arctic are migratory. They have particularly soft and dense down feathers for warmth, and the females pluck some of their breast feathers to line their nests. People use these feathers to fill pillows and quilts.

Atlantic puffin (*Fratercula arctica*)

Water lovers

Puffins spend most of their lives on the water and only come on land to breed and nest. They look ungainly on land, but are excellent swimmers, especially underwater when they are looking to catch fish.

Birds of the Antarctic

The most common Antarctic birds are seabirds such as penguins, albatrosses, and petrels. They come ashore to breed in summer when the seas around Antarctica are packed with food. Few flying species nest on the mainland, instead forming crowded colonies on nearby islands. Most leave in winter, but some stay to complete their long breeding cycle.

Seaweed nest

Blue-eyed shags nest in smelly, noisy colonies close to the sea, building untidy nests of seaweed, lichens, mosses, and feathers glued together with guano (bird poop). Some use these sites all year round, to roost near their fishing grounds.

Feathers soak up water and allow the shag to dive more easily.

Wings are held up high, making the bird appear large and fierce.

Skuas emit ear-splitting shrieks to warn off enemies.

Powerful, hooked beak stabs and kills prey.

Antarctic skua
(*Catharacta maccormicki*)

Pirates of the skies

Skuas live up to their reputation as "pirates of the skies" by chasing other birds and forcing them to regurgitate their food. These large, aggressive birds also steal the eggs and young of other birds.

Brown skua
(*Catharacta lonnbergi*)

Wings are spread out to dry off after a swim.

Jagged, hooked bill helps grip slippery fish as well as nest material.

Blue-eyed shag
(*Phalacrocorax atriceps*)

Antarctic scavengers

Giant petrels use their powerful, hooked beaks for feeding and scavenging, as well as killing other birds. These dangerous predators are about the size of vultures, with wingspans of nearly 6½ ft (2 m). They eat almost anything, including dead seals and whales.

Giant petrel
(*Macronectes giganteus*)

Horny sheath protects nostrils.

Sheathbill
(*Chionis albus*)

Not fussy

Sheathbills are the only land birds able to scrape a living year-round in Antarctica due to their varied diet, which includes penguin and seal feces, penguin eggs, chicks, dead fish, krill, and limpets.

Only **13 species** of flying bird **use** ice-free Antarctic **land for nesting**.

FISHING TECHNIQUES

Antarctic birds use different techniques to fish. Cormorants use their strong feet to paddle deep underwater, while penguins dive deep and then propel themselves using their wings. Terns dive just under the surface, while albatrosses float on the surface to pick out food. Shearwaters spot their prey from the air and then plunge in pursuit.

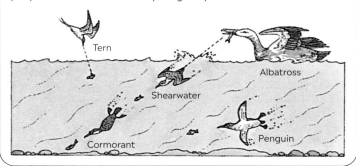

Tern
Albatross
Shearwater
Cormorant
Penguin

Ghostly hunter

Snowy owls feed largely on the millions of lemmings living in the Arctic tundra. Many of them wander far south in winter.

Snowy owl
(*Bubo scandiacus*)

Sky lords

The huge summer breeding colonies of birds in the Arctic and in Antarctica offer predatory birds easy meals of eggs and chicks. In the Arctic tundra, small mammals such as lemmings and hares increase the range of prey, so the Arctic has more predatory birds than the Antarctic. The predators breed at the same time as their prey, so their chicks have plenty to eat.

Feathers at tips of wings spread out like fingers to help the eagle push and steer through the air.

Broad wings give both speed and control in flight.

Strong legs cushion impact of landing.

The golden eagle slows in mid-air and spreads its wings and tail to act as a brake.

Eyes firmly focused on its destination, the eagle brakes its flight by swinging out its legs.

Lethal curved talons can grip, crush, and carry off prey.

At the last moment, its feet swing down to grip the perch.

Watch out

Golden eagles fly at low altitudes while hunting, then swoop to pounce on their prey. This swoop-and-grab attack happens swiftly and the prey is often taken unawares. Here, a golden eagle is landing on a branch in much the same way.

Golden eagle
(*Aquila chrysaetos*)

Sharp eyesight to spot birds and small mammals on the ground below.

Hooked bill can tear flesh from prey.

Enormous wings are powered by huge chest muscles.

Feathers down to toes keep feet warm.

Gyrfalcon
(*Falco rusticolus*)

A killing machine
The golden eagle is a superb flier, and hunts birds and small mammals. Its range extends widely across the northern hemisphere, and it even nests directly on the ground in tundra regions.

Biggest and best
The gyrfalcon, the most powerful of the falcons, relies on power and speed to catch its prey. Its usual victims include the rock ptarmigan or waterfowl, which the gyrfalcon might grab and kill while flying.

Ocean wanderer

The huge albatrosses of Antarctic seas come ashore only to breed, on islands to the north of the Antarctic mainland, such as South Georgia. Six species of albatross breed in the Antarctic: the black-browed, gray-headed, yellow-nosed, wandering, sooty, and light-mantled sooty. They raise only one chick at a time, which is slow to mature, staying in the nest for up to a year.

Long, slender wings allow effortless gliding over the ocean.

Bumpy landing
When these huge birds approach their nest site, they circle round several times before putting their legs down, and often land with a bump.

Black-browed albatross
(*Diomedea melanophris*)

Webbed feet push against the air and act as brakes.

Large eyes help spot food at sea.

Dead weight
In the poem *The Rime of the Ancient Mariner* (1798) by English poet Samuel Taylor Coleridge, a man who has killed an albatross is made to wear it around his neck as a sign of bad luck.

Due to their large wings and body weight, albatrosses need a run-up to gather speed for take-off.

Gray-headed albatross
(*Thalassarche chrysostoma*)

The high life
Gray-headed albatrosses live and nest on steep cliff sides, to take advantage of the strong winds rising over the cliffs for take-off. However, because of the harsh conditions, only half their chicks survive.

Hooked bill has razor-sharp edges to grip fish and squid.

During courtship, the bird points its beak to the sky and moos like a cow.

Faithful flying ace

The wandering albatross has the greatest wingspan of any living bird, enabling it to cover as much as 300 miles (500 km) a day. Like all albatrosses, it comes ashore only to breed. Its long breeding cycle takes a year to complete, and so it breeds only every two years. Wandering albatrosses usually pair for life, and new pairs perform an elaborate courtship dance with their partner.

Wandering albatross (*Diomedea exulans*)

Wingspan can be up to 11 ft (3.5 m).

Second-hand food

When parent albatrosses return to the nest after many hours or days fishing out at sea, they feed their young by bringing up their catch in the form of a sticky, oily mixture. They can also spit this smelly oil to repel predators such as skuas.

Mother feeds regurgitated krill to her chick.

Thick down feathers and layer of fat protect the chick from intense cold.

Barrel nest

The black-browed albatross makes a raised nest of mud and straw, lined with grass and feathers.

Penguin parade

Millions of penguins gather at their summer breeding colonies in Antarctica. The Adélie, emperor, and chinstrap penguins breed on the continent, while the gentoo, macaroni, rockhopper, and king penguins breed within Antarctic waters. Penguins rely on thick fat under their skin for energy when they are caring for eggs and chicks, and cannot get out to sea to feed.

Padded penguins
Tough feathers, flexible skin, and thick blubber protect these penguins as they hurl themselves onto rocky shores or ice floes.

Large colonies
Penguins breed in huge, densely packed colonies called rookeries. Some rookeries contain millions of birds.

Feathers along part of the beak provide warmth.

Torpedo-shaped body allows the bird to slice through the water.

Powerful flippers propel the penguin through the water.

Adélie penguin (*Pygoscelis adeliae*)

Oily feathers provide a waterproof layer for the thick down feathers beneath.

👁 EYEWITNESS

Stefan Christmann
German photographer Stefan Christmann has won awards for capturing the daily lives of emperor penguins in Antarctica in winter. His photographs show how penguins help each other survive and raise their young in freezing temperatures.

Long march
Adélies winter out at sea off the pack ice but march inland to their breeding colonies in October. They lay their eggs in November, and by February the chicks go to sea.

Short legs help steer while swimming.

Who's who?

A penguin's main distinguishing marks are on the head and upper breast. They use their colors and crests for species recognition and courtship displays.

King penguins have golden-orange patches on their head and bill. Their long bills help catch speedy fish and squid.

Gentoo penguins have pink, dagger-shaped bills to catch fish and krill. They can swim at speeds of 23 mph (36 kph).

Rockhoppers use their yellow eyebrows for courtship displays. They are the smallest polar penguin.

Noisy nesters

Chinstrap penguins are good climbers, using their beaks and sharp claws to reach nest sites in high, rocky places. Noisy and aggressive, they often take over Adélies' nesting sites or steal stones from one another's nests.

Black feathers form a "chinstrap" across the white throat.

Predation

Predators, such as skuas, snatch penguin eggs and chicks. At sea, penguins are prey to leopard seals, killer whales, and sea lions.

Chinstrap penguin (*Pygoscelis antarctica*)

Emperor penguin
(*Aptenodytes forsteri*)

Emperors of the Antarctic

In early April, the emperor penguins of Antarctica begin a 60-mile (100-km) trek south, in pitch darkness, to reach their nesting sites on the pack ice. In early May, just before the start of the southern winter, the females lay eggs and return to the open sea. In an incredible feat of endurance, the males incubate the eggs for two months during the icy winter, until the females return to feed the hatched chicks in July. Emperor pairs rear one chick each year but only about one out of five survives.

Feet are small to cut down on heat loss.

Feet heat
Chicks stand on the adults' feet for the first eight weeks, hiding under a brood pouch (flap of skin) for warmth. Older chicks stay warm by relying on their dense, fluffy feathers and the warm bodies of fellow chicks.

Majestic

The largest penguin of all, the emperor stands nearly 4 ft (about 1.15 m) tall, and weighs 65 lb (30 kg). It can spend up to 18 minutes underwater and dive to more than 850 ft (260 m). In 2018, an emperor penguin dive was recorded that lasted more than 30 minutes to a depth of 1,640 ft (500 m).

Closely packed, overlapping feathers cover a thick layer of blubber.

Some emperor penguin colonies contain more than 20,000 pairs.

Birds take turns occupying the most exposed position.

DUCKING AND DIVING

Penguins "fly" through the water propelled by their stiff flippers. When swimming fast, they often use a technique called porpoising—leaping out of the water like dolphins or porpoises—and can travel at speeds of 18 mph (30 kph).

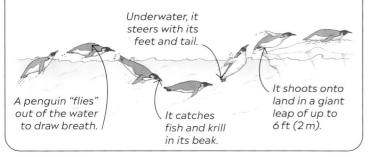

Underwater, it steers with its feet and tail.

A penguin "flies" out of the water to draw breath.

It catches fish and krill in its beak.

It shoots onto land in a giant leap of up to 6 ft (2 m).

Togetherness

Incubating males huddle for warmth, moving very little to conserve energy and keeping their backs turned toward the constantly shifting winds. A tightly packed group can reduce heat loss by as much as 50 percent.

King of the **Arctic**

Polar bears are among the largest and most powerful hunters in the Arctic, and the only land mammals that can live out on sea ice. They are solitary except in the breeding season. Their dense fur keeps them warm in the most severe of conditions. An undercoat of thick fur is protected by an outer coat of long guard hairs, which stick together when wet to form a waterproof barrier. Under the fur, a thick layer of blubber insulates the bear against the cold, and acts as a food store in hard times.

Small, rounded ears reduce loss of body heat.

Mature female polar bear (*Ursus maritimus*)

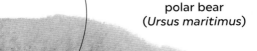

Heavyweight

An average adult male polar bear measures 8 ft (2.5 m) from head to tail and weighs more than 1,000 lb (500 kg). The largest males grow up to 10 ft (3 m) in length and can weigh up to 2,000 lb (900 kg). Females are much smaller than the males.

Play fighting

Young bears often wrestle in the snow. Play helps strengthen the cubs and lets them practice the skills they will need as adults.

Air vent in the roof lets stale air escape.

Females dig the tunnel, then hollow out the chamber.

Cave cubs

Cubs are born in December or January in a warm, cozy den dug in the snow by their mother. Cubs grow rapidly on the mother's rich milk, while the mother lives on the stored fat in her body.

Polar bear island

Wrangel Island in the Russian Arctic is also known as the "polar bear maternity ward." This small island has the greatest number of polar bear dens in the world, and every year up to 600 female polar bears give birth to cubs on the island.

Polar paddle

Polar bears swim slowly but strongly, and can keep swimming for days. They use only their front legs to swim, while the back legs are held still like a rudder.

Patient hunters

Seals make up more than 90 percent of the polar bear diet. Polar bears wait near breathing holes in the sea ice and pounce when seals come up for air. Only some hunting trips are successful and a bear may not eat for many weeks or months.

Fur often appears yellowish.

Hollow hairs trap warm air near body.

Thickly padded soles are covered by rough skin and sometimes tough hair.

Sharp claws

Nonslip soles help grip slippery ice.

Mighty **moose**

The moose is the largest member of the deer family, and can be more than 7 ft (2.4 m) tall. It is found across northern Canada and the United States, as well as northern Europe and Asia, where it is also called an elk. In Europe and Asia, moose live mainly in coniferous forests bordering the tundra, while some North American populations are known to range widely over the tundra. Because of their size, these animals need a large area to themselves to find an adequate food supply. In winter, herds of moose often travel great distances in search of food.

Lethal weapons
Male (bull) moose use their heavy, flattened antlers to fight rival males in the breeding season. They shed their antlers every year and grow a new set.

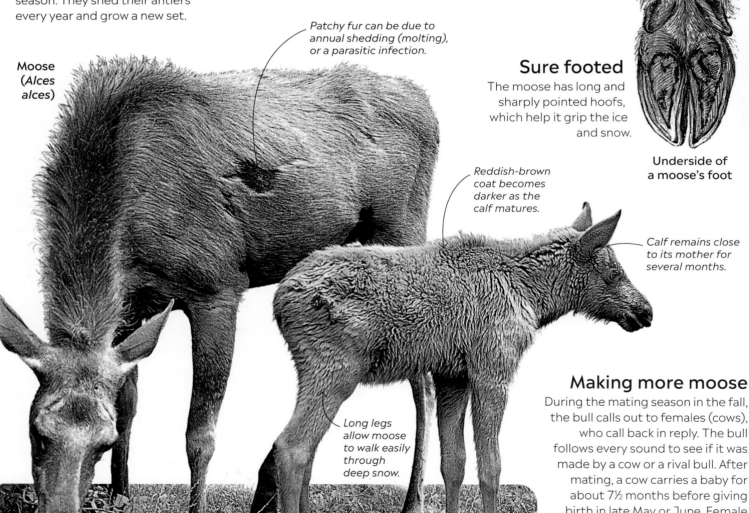

Patchy fur can be due to annual shedding (molting), or a parasitic infection.

Moose
(*Alces alces*)

Reddish-brown coat becomes darker as the calf matures.

Sure footed
The moose has long and sharply pointed hoofs, which help it grip the ice and snow.

Underside of a moose's foot

Calf remains close to its mother for several months.

Long legs allow moose to walk easily through deep snow.

Making more moose
During the mating season in the fall, the bull calls out to females (cows), who call back in reply. The bull follows every sound to see if it was made by a cow or a rival bull. After mating, a cow carries a baby for about 7½ months before giving birth in late May or June. Female moose usually have just one calf, although twins and even triplets are not uncommon. When the calf is about 10 days old, it can travel with its mother.

Antlers can spread to as much as 6 ft (1.8 m).

Antlers are not fully grown and have a "velvet" covering that falls off later.

An adult male moose can weigh up to 1,815 lb (825 kg).

Long muzzle hangs 3–4 in (8–10 cm) over the chin.

Arctic willow (*Salix arctica*)

Favorite food
The Alaska and Arctic willow plants are favorites in the moose's diet.

Solitary giant
In the tundra, the moose's preferred habitat is land with willow swamps and lakes. Moose are good swimmers and can cross lakes and rivers with ease. In summer, they eat leaves and tender twigs, as well as grass and herbs. Wolves occasionally attack isolated moose and young, but thanks to their great size and dangerous antlers, moose have few other natural predators apart from humans.

With its long legs and short neck, the moose has to get on its knees to eat low-growing plants.

Water waders
Standing up to their knees in water helps moose get rid of flies that plague them during the warm summer. Moose also feed on aquatic vegetation, with an adult able to eat up to 43 lb (19.5 kg) of it in a day.

Tundra life

During the Arctic summer, much of the snow on the tundra melts, plants begin to grow, and insects hatch. Now there is plenty of food for animals that live on the tundra, as well as the migrants that arrive when the weather warms. These animals breed and raise their young as quickly as possible, because the summer is short and the land soon freezes over again.

Tundra vegetation

The tundra has an almost continuous cover of vegetation. Grasslike flowering plants, called sedges—such as Arctic cotton grass (*Eriophorum angustifolium*), above—predominate, together with true grasses. Scattered among them are mosses, flowering herbs, and dwarf shrubs and willows.

Coat is extra thick in winter.

Long, pointed ears enable the lynx to hear well in dense, muffling snow.

Feline visitor

The Canada lynx (*Lynx canadensis*) lives mainly in forests bordering areas of tundra in North America, but it is often to be found in the true tundra in summer. It preys almost entirely on snowshoe hares.

Hare line

Three types of hare inhabit the tundra—the snowshoe, Alaskan, and Arctic. They use their well-developed claws to dig, even through snow, for food. These hares grow white coats in winter.

Snowshoe hare
(*Lepus americanus*)

SEA OF ICE

The central area of the Arctic Ocean is permanently frozen. The surrounding tundra is covered in snow and ice in winter, but is lush in summer. Few trees grow on the tundra due to extreme cold and strong winds.

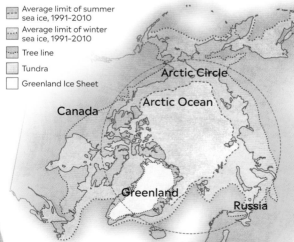

- Average limit of summer sea ice, 1991–2010
- Average limit of winter sea ice, 1991–2010
- Tree line
- Tundra
- Greenland Ice Sheet

Arctic Circle

Arctic Ocean

Canada

Greenland

Russia

Speedy stalker

A ruthless hunter, the stoat's sleek shape allows it to move quickly, pursuing prey into burrows, crevices, and even underground tunnels. Stoats turn white during winter to blend in with the landscape.

Stoat (*Mustela erminea*)

Ferocious carnivore

A distant relative of the stoat, the wolverine looks like a small bear. Wolverines are solitary and usually meet others only to mate in summer. They are relentless hunters, pursuing their prey for miles. They eat most of their kill on the spot, but hide the rest for later.

Wolverine (*Gulo gulo*)

Fur is occasionally tipped silvery white.

Bears have sensitive noses and a strong sense of smell.

Powerful jaws and teeth allow bears to eat a variety of foods.

Sleepyhead

The brown bear (*Ursus arctos*) has a wide geographical range, including the tundra regions in Alaska, Canada, and parts of Russia. It eats a wide variety of small mammals, fish, insects, and plants, depending on what is available. Brown bears hibernate in winter in snug dens in the ground, living off their reserves of stored fat. They sometimes sleep for up to seven months.

Long claws on the front paws help the bear dig.

Reindeer and caribou

Wild reindeer survive on the frozen tundra of North America (where they are called caribou), Scandinavia, and Siberia, but they have also been domesticated in Scandinavia and Siberia for thousands of years. Although their thick coats insulate them against the Arctic cold, many populations migrate south in the winter to find food and shelter.

Title fight
In the fall mating (rutting) season, male reindeer (bulls) wrestle, with their antlers locked together to decide who is the strongest. The winner collects a group of females (cows) for mating, and then defends his harem against all challengers.

BIG ANTLERS

Reindeer shed their antlers every year. Bulls shed their antlers in winter, and cows in spring. New antlers grow rapidly and are fully grown by the start of the fall mating season. Although reindeer grow large, heavy antlers, they do not use them for defense, relying instead on their speed to flee from predators.

Antler buds appear two weeks after the old ones are shed.

New antlers are covered by soft, thick velvet.

Fully formed antlers are hard as bone.

Reindeer are the only deer in which both sexes grow antlers.

Reindeer molt their thick outer winter coats as warmer weather approaches.

Strong swimmers

Migrating reindeer have to cross many fast-flowing, often icy, rivers. Their broad feet help them swim strongly against the current, and the hollow hairs in their coats help them float more easily.

Reindeer herding

Reindeer herding is the primary source of livelihood for more than 20 Indigenous Arctic and subarctic peoples. Many Indigenous reindeer herders live alongside their herds for most of the year, following their migration routes throughout the seasons, looking for viable pastures.

Calf grows its first antlers at around 2 months.

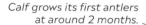

Growing up fast

Calves are born in June and grow fast on their mother's rich milk, which is four times as nutritious as cow's milk. They can keep up with the herd when they are just one or two days old, which helps protect them from predators. Calves stay with their mothers for about a year.

Dense coat turns gray-white in winter.

Sharp hoofs grip ice and dig through snow for food.

👁 EYEWITNESS

Manuela Panzacchi
Italian research scientist Manuela Panzacchi studies how the changing Arctic environment affects wild reindeer. She also tracks the shifting migratory patterns of reindeer, and their impact on Indigenous communities that rely on reindeer for subsistence.

Lichen lunch

Reindeer feed largely on lichens, which are one of the few foods available throughout the long Arctic winter. Some reindeer living on Arctic islands also eat seaweed. In summer, a wider variety of plants is available. Adult reindeer eat about 10 lb (4.5 kg) of food a day to get the energy they need.

Arctic wolf
(*Canis lupus arctos*)

Company of **wolves**

Wolves are intelligent, adaptable animals with a wide natural range. Arctic populations rely on their thick fur and cooperative hunting to survive. They live in packs of up to 20 family members, led by the elder mother and father. Each pack ranges over a specific area, picking off sick, aged, or injured herd animals. Although wolves may be feared by humans, they kill only to survive.

Blending in

In Arctic areas of North America and Eurasia, wolves often have white coats for camouflage, so they can get close to their prey undetected. In forests south of the tundra, wolves have gray or blackish fur.

Ring of horns

Wolves are expert hunters and prey chiefly on large hoofed animals such as caribou, moose, and musk oxen. To defend themselves, a herd of musk oxen forms a tight circle, with the females and young in the center. An attacking wolf can be caught by musk oxen horns, tossed into the air, and then trampled.

Wolf throws back its head in order to howl.

Pack life

Most wolf packs consist of two parents and their cubs. A pack may also include older offspring of the parent pair, who have not yet headed out on their own. Younger wolves are submissive to the parents, who lead the pack in hunting and control the supply of food. Wolf pairs stay together for life.

In harmony

Wolf-speak ranges from whimpers and growls to complex facial and body expressions. Howling is just one of the ways wolves communicate with each other. It is used to keep in touch with pack members, or to warn other packs away from their area. If one wolf howls, the others join in, with a variety of sound that makes the pack seem bigger and more formidable.

Born to be wild

Wolves are well adapted to Arctic life. Their keen senses of smell and hearing are perfect for tracking down their prey. Agile and graceful, they can jump up to 15 ft (4.5 m) and can leap upward, sideways, and even backward, much like a cat. Their feet have large pads with claws that do not retract, allowing them to run fast on flat ground and keep their footing on rocks, ice, and other slippery surfaces.

Two-layered coat with soft, dense underfur and long, outer hairs keeps out the cold.

Wolves have evolved long legs and strong bodies for chasing down their prey.

Long muzzle hides powerful jaws and teeth capable of killing prey and tearing flesh.

Gray wolf (*Canis lupus*)

The gray wolf is the ancestor of domesticated dogs.

Caring for cubs

The female of a pack usually gives birth to 4–6 cubs in a den, which is a rocky cave or a hole in the ground. The cubs are born blind and deaf, and have grayish-brown coats that help conceal them in the dens. The cubs are cared for by the whole pack, and the mother feeds them a diet of regurgitated meat. They start to leave the den after about 5 weeks, but only begin traveling with the pack after they are 12 weeks old.

 EYEWITNESS

Dr. L. David Mech

US wolf biologist David Mech spent more than 20 summers studying Arctic wolves on Ellesmere Island, Canada, where the wolves have little fear of humans because they have never been hunted. His observations show that pack leaders become dominant because they are usually the only pair that breeds.

The walrus

The huge and ungainly walrus, a close relative of seals, is superbly adapted to its Arctic lifestyle. Four flat flippers make it an excellent swimmer, and allow it to shift its bulk on land. A thick layer of blubber keeps the animal warm. Walruses follow the seasonal advance and retreat of the Arctic ice, migrating as far as 1,860 miles (3,000 km) every time. Along the way, they must evade polar bears and killer whales—their only predators.

Famous walrus

In *Alice Through the Looking Glass* by English author Lewis Carroll (1832–1898), a walrus and a carpenter eat oysters. In reality, walruses eat other bivalve shellfish, such as mussels and clams.

The call of love

During mating season, male walruses woo females with barks, growls, and whistles. If the female is impressed, she will mate with the male in the water. Females produce a calf every other spring, usually on a boulder-strewn beach, and care for their young for two years.

Intensely sociable

In summer, walruses lie around on dry land, packed together in large, noisy groups called pods. Keeping close conserves body heat and makes it harder for predators to pick off individuals.

A walrus can **slow its heartbeat** to allow it **to dive** into the icy waters of the Arctic.

Thick skin on the upper body protects the walrus during fights.

Blubber may be more than 4 in (10 cm) thick.

Walrus
(*Odobenus rosmarus*)

Carved animals decorate the tusk.

Game board carved from a walrus tusk

Walrus ivory is harder than elephant ivory.

Multipurpose animal

The Inuit have always hunted walruses because every part of the animal is useful to them. The meat, blubber, skin, and organs are a rich source of food, the hides are processed into rope or used to cover boats, and the ivory tusks are hand carved into jewelery, artwork, and other handicrafts.

Heave ho!

During winter and spring, walruses spend much of their time drifting along on large floating fields of ice. They use their tusks as ice picks to heave themselves out of the water, flopping belly-down onto the ice.

Heavy skull protects brain when animal smashes though ice up to 9 in (22 cm) thick.

Mustache of coarse but sensitive whiskers, used in search for invertebrate prey.

Long tusks

The tusks of the walrus are actually its upper canine teeth, which point downward, and grow as long as 3 ft (1 m). A walrus uses its tusks to rake up the sea floor in search of food, to fight rivals during the breeding season, and to defend itself against predators.

Lower jaw

A walrus can stab larger prey with its tusks, but it eats mainly shellfish.

Both male and female walruses have tusks.

Broad front flippers support the heavy body on land.

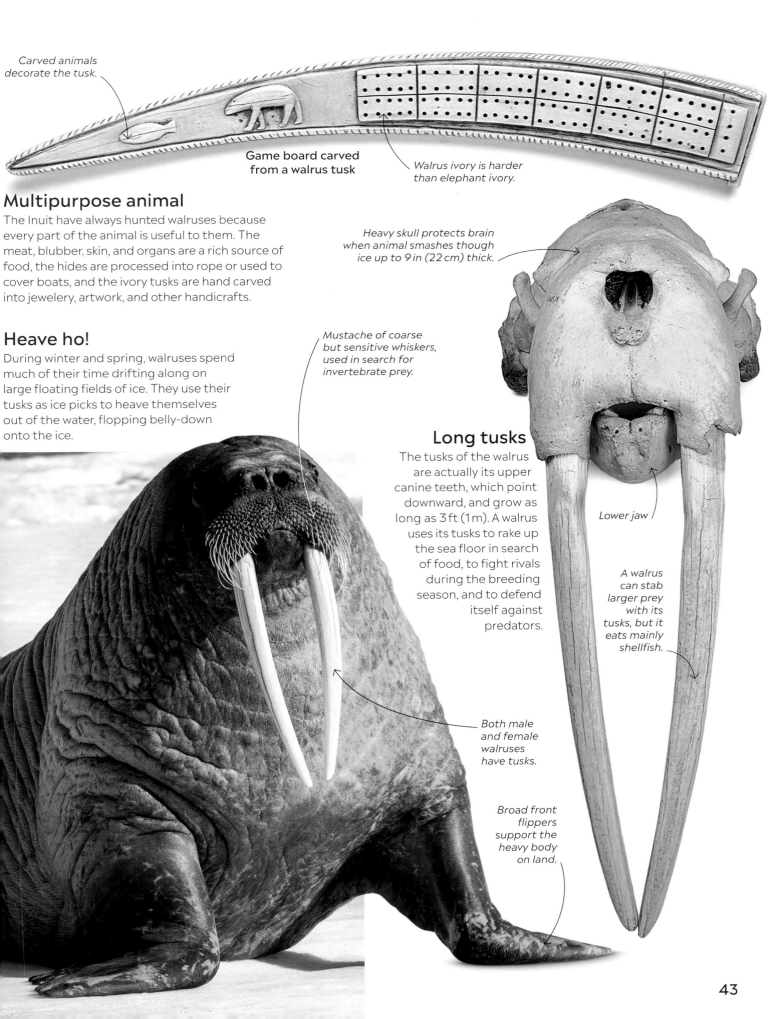

Suited to the sea

Seals may be the hardiest of all polar mammals. The Arctic ringed seal and the Antarctic Weddell seal survive below the ice during winter, while others, such as the Arctic harp seal, migrate into polar waters in summer. All seals leave the water to mate and give birth, and to rest. In contrast to their graceful swimming in the sea, they move clumsily on land. Seals have been hunted for their fur and blubber for centuries. Today, seal populations are increasingly threatened by the rising pollution in the oceans.

Guard hairs protect the seal as it slides over rocks on land.

Dense underfur traps a layer of warm air and keeps the seal warm.

Two fur coats
Fur seals have long guard hairs on the outside and dense underfur. Many seals have hairless bodies, and depend on their blubber for warmth.

Icy winters
The Weddell seal (*Leptonychotes weddellii*), spends winter under the Antarctic sea ice, gnawing at it to keep air holes open for breathing. These seals can dive to about 1,900 ft (580 m), and can stay submerged for up to 70 minutes.

Balloon nose
The Arctic male hooded seal (*Cystophora cristata*) has a balloon-like structure at the end of its nose, which it inflates to warn off rivals or enemies.

Huge swollen nose like an elephant's trunk

Jobs for the boys
The gigantic male southern elephant seal (*Mirounga leonina*) roars defiance to its rivals in the breeding season, using its extraordinary nose like a loudspeaker. Males do not eat during the breeding season, since they are constantly defending a harem of females against rivals. Females give birth to a single pup, which they suckle for about a month. They also do not feed during this time, surviving instead on energy from their blubber.

Males are up to 10 times heavier than females.

Pups quadruple in weight during the 3–4 weeks they are suckled.

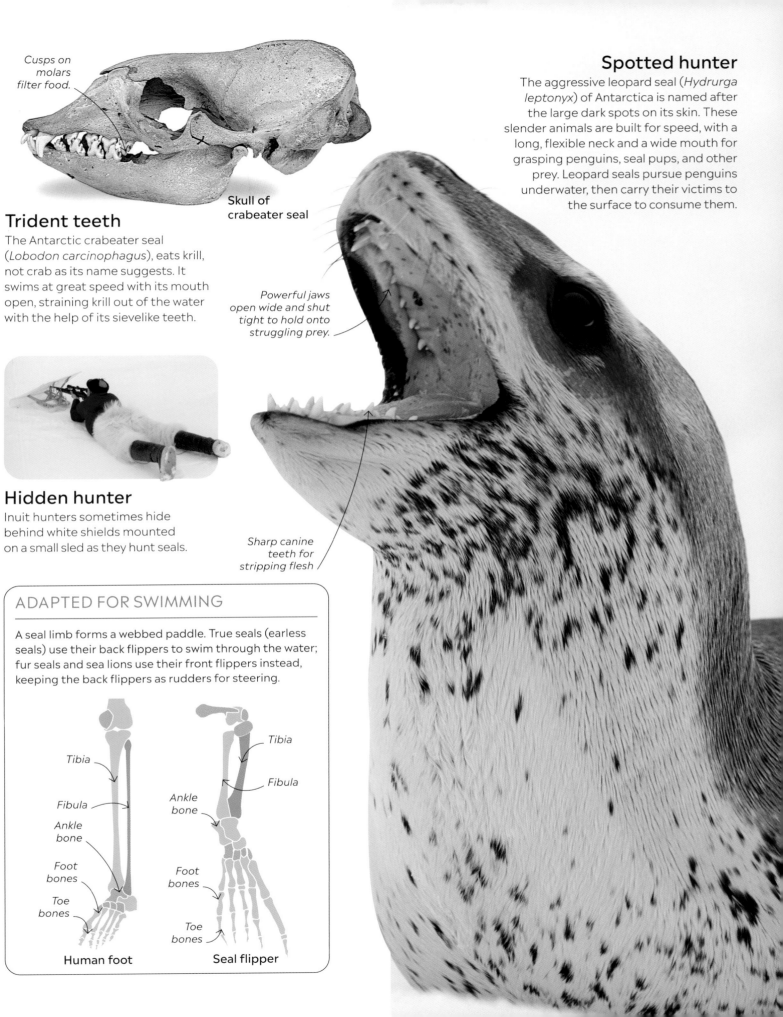

Cusps on molars filter food.

Skull of crabeater seal

Trident teeth

The Antarctic crabeater seal (*Lobodon carcinophagus*), eats krill, not crab as its name suggests. It swims at great speed with its mouth open, straining krill out of the water with the help of its sievelike teeth.

Hidden hunter

Inuit hunters sometimes hide behind white shields mounted on a small sled as they hunt seals.

Spotted hunter

The aggressive leopard seal (*Hydrurga leptonyx*) of Antarctica is named after the large dark spots on its skin. These slender animals are built for speed, with a long, flexible neck and a wide mouth for grasping penguins, seal pups, and other prey. Leopard seals pursue penguins underwater, then carry their victims to the surface to consume them.

Powerful jaws open wide and shut tight to hold onto struggling prey.

Sharp canine teeth for stripping flesh

ADAPTED FOR SWIMMING

A seal limb forms a webbed paddle. True seals (earless seals) use their back flippers to swim through the water; fur seals and sea lions use their front flippers instead, keeping the back flippers as rudders for steering.

Tibia

Fibula

Ankle bone

Foot bones

Toe bones

Tibia

Fibula

Ankle bone

Foot bones

Toe bones

Human foot

Seal flipper

Giants of
the seas

Polar seas are home to a whole range of whales. Gray, humpback, fin, and blue whales are summer residents, feasting on a rich supply of plankton. When winter comes, most of them migrate to warmer waters near the equator. Narwhal, beluga, and bowhead whales remain in the Arctic all year round, while minke whales are able to survive the Antarctic winter.

Sea unicorn

The spiral, ivory tusk of the male narwhal (*Monodon monoceros*) is an elongated tooth. While Indigenous peoples have always hunted narwhals for subsistence, male narwhals have been hunted by Europeans for their tusks for centuries.

Long haul

Gray whales make the longest migration journeys of any whale. They breed off the coasts of California and Mexico in winter, then swim to their Alaskan feeding grounds for the summer, a round trip of more than 12,000 miles (20,000 km). Gray whales only feed in the summer, living off stores of energy in their blubber for the rest of the year.

Blow hole on top of head closes underwater.

Gray whale
(*Eschrichtius robustus*)

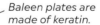

Top attaches to whale's upper jaw.

Baleen plates are made of keratin.

Giant sieves

Some whales, such as the humpback, right, gray, and blue whales, sieve food from the sea water using fringed brushes called baleen inside their mouths. These whales have huge, arched jaws from which the baleen plates hang like curtains.

👁 EYEWITNESS

Dr. Roger Payne

In 1967, US biologist Roger Payne (1935–2023) realized that the underwater sounds recorded by an engineer were whale songs. He released these recordings to inspire interest in whale conservation. Dr. Payne also played a vital role in ending commercial whale hunting.

The big one

The blue whale is the largest animal alive today. It was once close to extinction because of commercial overhunting, but numbers are now recovering.

Blue whale
(*Balaenoptera musculus*)

Sperm whale (*Physeter macrocephalus*)

Back has a row of 6–14 humps, but no dorsal fin.

Champion diver

Sperm whales are known to dive to great depths and hold their breath for a long time. They can dive to about 9,842 ft (3,000 m) for up to 2 hours.

Large, strong muscles in the tail power the flukes.

Flat, rigid tail flukes move up and down to push the whale through the water.

Barnacles often cling to the whale's skin.

Fast killers

Killer whales (*Orcinus orca*), also known as orcas, live in pods of 4–40 individuals that hunt together. They are the fastest mammals in the sea, able to plow through water at 35 mph (56 kph).

NATURAL BALANCE

Orcas are the top carnivore in many subarctic and subantarctic food chains, because they hunt fish, seals, penguins, and other whales. Humans often come into conflict with orcas because they feel these whales take valuable fish stocks. However, killer whales are a vital part of the food webs of the polar seas because they help keep the natural balance of life in the oceans.

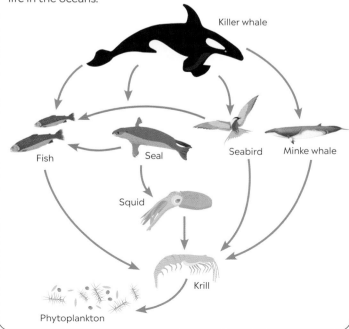

Killer whale

Fish

Seal

Seabird

Minke whale

Squid

Krill

Phytoplankton

A herding life

In Eurasia's Arctic regions, Indigenous peoples have followed a nomadic (traveling) hunting, herding, and fishing lifestyle for thousands of years, adapting to the intense winter cold and darkness. These peoples include the Sámi of the Scandinavian and Kola peninsulas in Europe, and the Chukchi, Evenks, and Nenets of Siberia and northeastern Asia. Today, they continue to pass on their traditional knowledge and culture, while also using new technologies. While some still herd reindeer, the majority, who now live in villages and towns, hold community festivals that support full-time reindeer herders.

Traveling bag
The northern Komi people, who live west of the Ural mountains in Russia, use *patkus*, or bags, like this one to carry clothes and other small items when following reindeer herds.

Reindeer provide people in the Arctic with **food, tents, clothes,** and **goods for trade.**

Model of a Nenets tent from Siberia

Moving camp
Nomadic people often move several times a year, so the dwellings they use are simple and lightweight yet sturdy. Their tents are made of a framework of wooden poles covered with reindeer skins. Openings are created near the top of the structure to let out smoke from fires.

Handy in winter

Indigenous peoples use reindeer as pack and draft (pulling) animals for carrying their goods. Reindeer herders might even rent out their reindeer sleds during the winter. Only a small number of reindeer from a herd are trained to pull sleds.

Hide from different parts of the reindeer body provides the changes of color in the decoration.

Hood is vital for keeping the head and ears warm in freezing conditions.

Seams are very finely stitched to make the garment as warm and waterproof as possible.

Mittens are sewn into the sleeves for extra warmth and protection.

Staying warm

The traditional winter coat of the Nenets people of northern Siberia consists of a thick, warm, long-sleeved jacket called a parka, sewn together from pieces of reindeer skin. Reindeer hide is worn on the outside, while softer fur is worn inside, next to the skin for extra warmth.

Sámi boots

These traditional Sámi boots are made of reindeer skin taken from the head and legs of the animal. They are worn with either traditional dried grass linings or felt boot liners. The flexible and light boots keep the wearer warm in harsh Arctic conditions.

Nenets child's hooded winter parka

Fur trim protects against icy winds.

Inuit carving of a woman standing on a seal, from Baffin Island

Hunters of the north

Inuit and Yupiit are the original inhabitants of the Arctic tundra of northern Canada, Alaska, Russia, and Greenland. As nomadic hunter-gatherers, they have traditionally lived near the coast in summer, building up food reserves for the winter, and traveled the rest of the year, hunting caribou, seals, polar bears, and whales. Most now live permanently in villages, towns, and cities, but often combine a regular job with hunting trips, which remain central to their way of life.

Inuit clothing is often richly embroidered.

Hunting seals

Marine mammals, including seals, are an important source of nutrition for Inuit and Yupiit across the North American Arctic. Depending on the location, Indigenous hunters may harvest ringed, harp, spotted, and bearded seals, among other species.

Inuit art

Historically, Inuit artists used walrus ivory, caribou antlers, and whale or seal bone from hunted animals to create elaborate carvings and sculptures. Today, Inuit artists work in a variety of traditional and contemporary materials and media, including sculpture, printmaking, drawing, and painting.

Only the tiniest area is exposed to the freezing air.

Sealskin jacket protects the hunter from icy Arctic winds.

Hunter pulls on a leather rope attached to the harpoon to haul a seal out of the water.

Inflated seal bladder is attached to a large catch so that it floats behind the canoe.

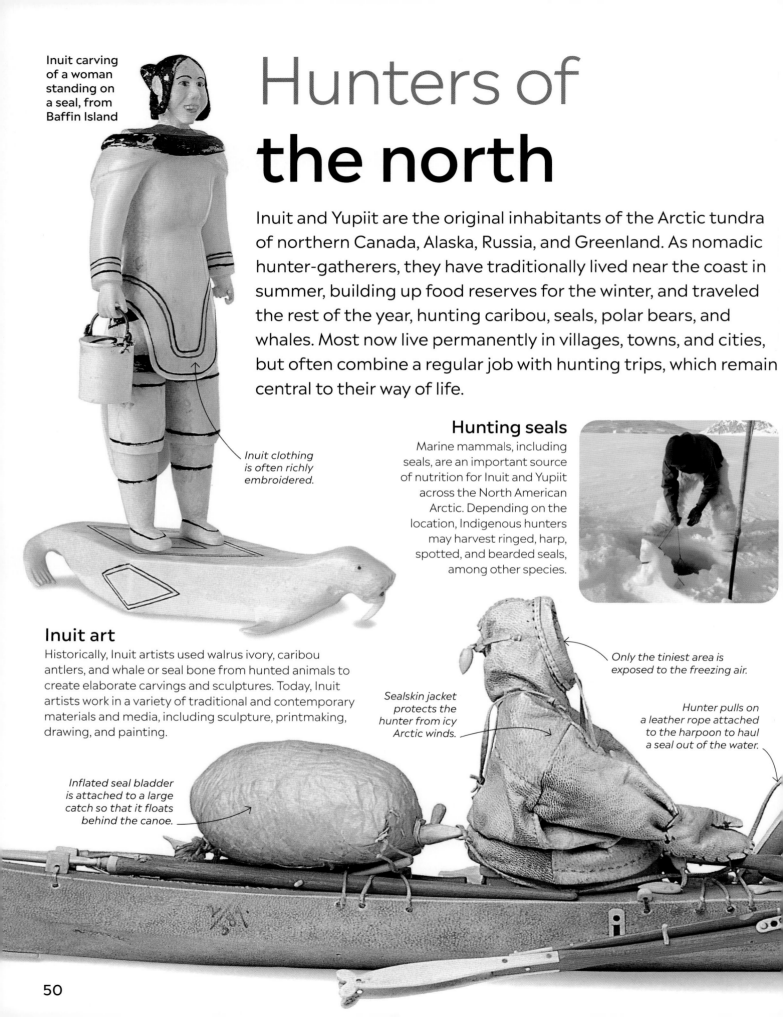

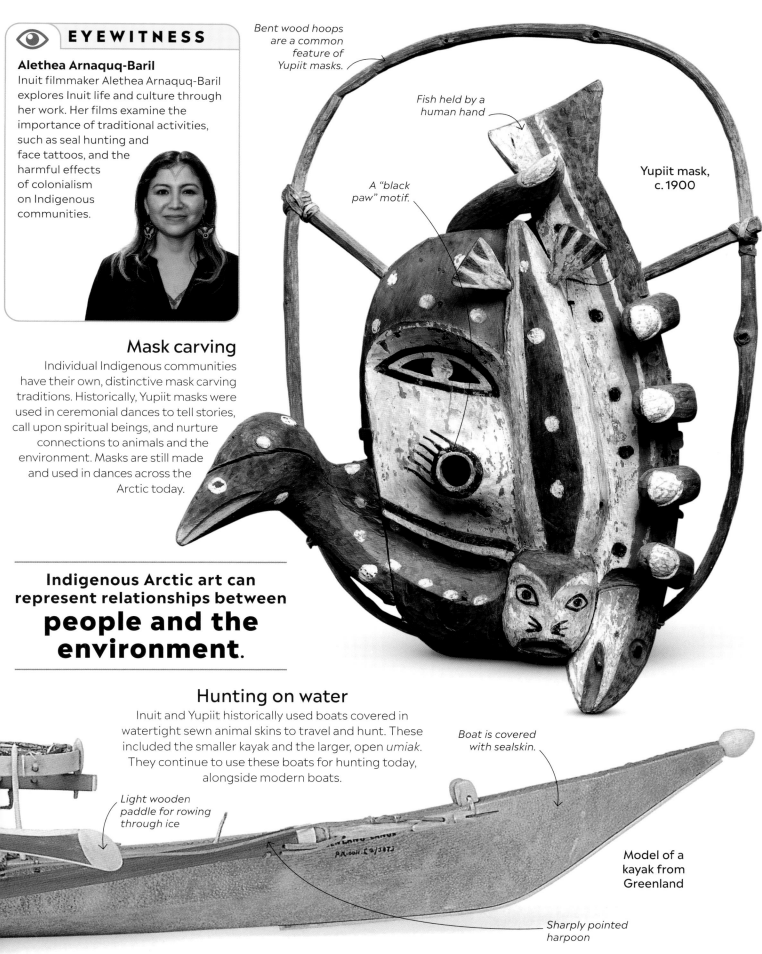

Mask carving

Individual Indigenous communities have their own, distinctive mask carving traditions. Historically, Yupiit masks were used in ceremonial dances to tell stories, call upon spiritual beings, and nurture connections to animals and the environment. Masks are still made and used in dances across the Arctic today.

Indigenous Arctic art can represent relationships between **people and the environment**.

Bent wood hoops are a common feature of Yupiit masks.

Fish held by a human hand

A "black paw" motif.

Yupiit mask, c. 1900

Hunting on water

Inuit and Yupiit historically used boats covered in watertight sewn animal skins to travel and hunt. These included the smaller kayak and the larger, open *umiak*. They continue to use these boats for hunting today, alongside modern boats.

Light wooden paddle for rowing through ice

Boat is covered with sealskin.

Model of a kayak from Greenland

Sharply pointed harpoon

European explorers

Balloon expedition

Salomon Andrée of Sweden tried to reach the North Pole by balloon in 1897, but it crashed, killing all on board.

Norwegian flag

From the 15th century, Europeans searched for a northern sea route to China and India that would reduce the time and danger involved in traveling overland. While the British and French explored a Northwest Passage along the northern North American coast, the Dutch and Russians concentrated on a Northeast Passage along the Siberian coast. Over the next 350 years, European sailors attempted to find their way through the Arctic.

Safe passage

In 1878, Swedish explorer Adolf Nordenskiöld made the first successful crossing of the Northeast Passage. In 1903, Norwegian explorer Roald Amundsen and his crew set out to navigate the Northwest Passage on a fishing boat called the *Gjøa*. They spent two years on King William Island, also known as Qikiqtaq, learning from the local Inuit community and collecting scientific data. In 1906, the *Gjøa* set off again and completed its journey.

Medals featuring an Arctic fox were given to people who helped search for the Franklin expedition.

The searchers

In 1847, British explorer John Franklin's expedition of 128 men was lost on its way through the Arctic. Numerous search teams set out to look for it. Although Franklin's crew perished, the information collected by the search parties helped advance European knowledge of the region.

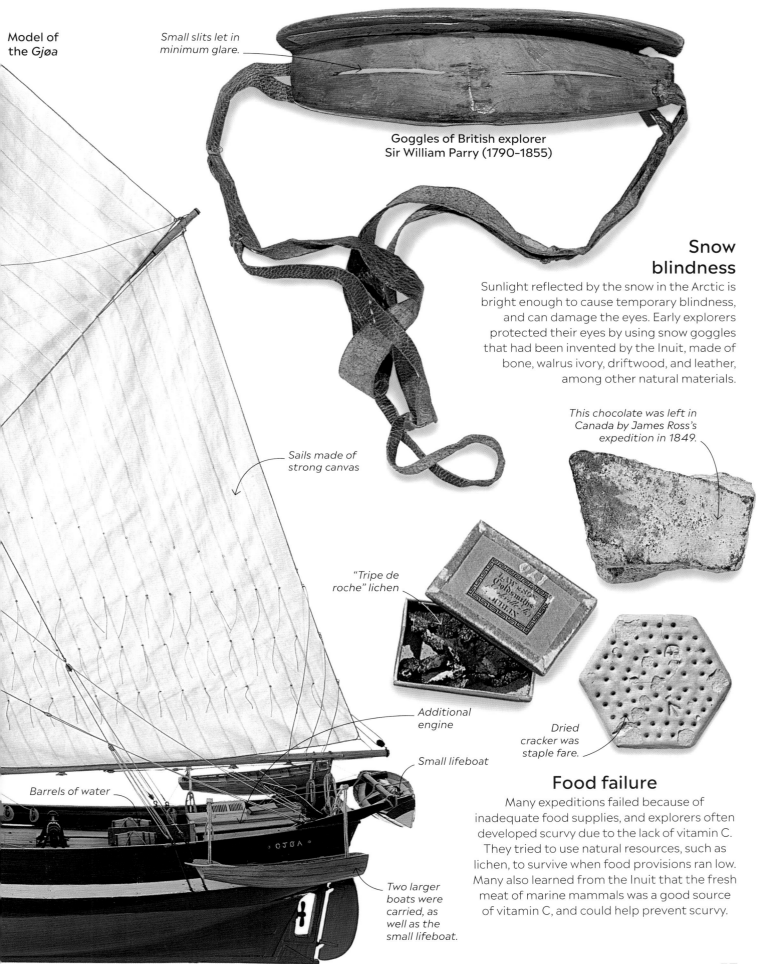

Model of the *Gjøa*

Small slits let in minimum glare.

Goggles of British explorer
Sir William Parry (1790–1855)

Snow blindness

Sunlight reflected by the snow in the Arctic is bright enough to cause temporary blindness, and can damage the eyes. Early explorers protected their eyes by using snow goggles that had been invented by the Inuit, made of bone, walrus ivory, driftwood, and leather, among other natural materials.

This chocolate was left in Canada by James Ross's expedition in 1849.

Sails made of strong canvas

"Tripe de roche" lichen

Additional engine

Small lifeboat

Dried cracker was staple fare.

Barrels of water

Two larger boats were carried, as well as the small lifeboat.

Food failure

Many expeditions failed because of inadequate food supplies, and explorers often developed scurvy due to the lack of vitamin C. They tried to use natural resources, such as lichen, to survive when food provisions ran low. Many also learned from the Inuit that the fresh meat of marine mammals was a good source of vitamin C, and could help prevent scurvy.

Race for the pole

In the early 20th century, European nations raced to explore Antarctica. In 1910, British naval officer Robert F. Scott set out for the South Pole. After using motorized sleds, ponies, and dogs through the harsh polar terrain, Scott and five companions arrived at the pole on January 17, 1912, only to find that the Norwegian explorer Roald Amundsen had reached it weeks before them. Scott and his men perished on the return journey.

Running repairs

Repairing cotton and canvas clothing was essential in polar conditions. This sewing kit is from Scott's 1910–1912 expedition.

Compact, lightweight kit for traveling

Microscope magnifies the image inside the instrument.

Side mirror reflects light into the instrument.

Günther & Tegetmeyer
BRAUNSCHWEIG, NO 4716

Base camp

From this desk at his base camp at Cape Evans, Scott (1868–1912) wrote his diary, letters, and reports, studied maps, and planned the details of his trek to the pole.

Electric research

Scott's team used this electrometer to measure tiny fluctuations in atmospheric electricity. Their expedition lost the race to the South Pole but their observations formed a new landmark in Antarctic science.

Wire to ground the instrument

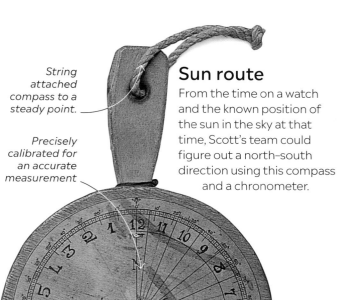

Sun route

String attached compass to a steady point.

Precisely calibrated for an accurate measurement

From the time on a watch and the known position of the sun in the sky at that time, Scott's team could figure out a north–south direction using this compass and a chronometer.

Pocket hospital

A tiny medical kit was vital on polar expeditions. Frostbite and injuries had to be treated quickly in the harsh conditions.

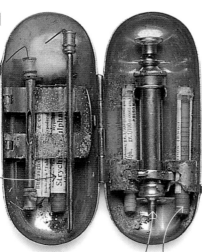

Poisons such as strychnine were used for medicinal purposes.

Syringe for administering standard doses of medicine

Tablets of painkillers such as morphine

Instrument made mostly of brass so not affected by magnetic fields

First to the pole

Amundsen (1872–1928) chose a shorter route to the pole than Scott, starting closer to the pole from a base camp at Framheim on the Ross Ice Shelf. His team of expert skiers and navigators was better prepared for fast travel, took along more food, and relied heavily on their dogs, especially for transportation.

Flying the flag

Amundsen set out for the South Pole in October 1911, reaching it on December 14, beating Scott by just over a month. Amundsen had learned about traveling in extreme cold from the Inuit of the Arctic. He was lost in a rescue mission in the Arctic in 1928.

ANTARCTICA

South Pole

Transantarctic Mountains

Ross Ice Shelf

Scott's last camp

Framheim ●

● Cape Evans

Ross Sea

———— Amundsen's route

———— Scott's route

Life in the **Arctic**

Many groups of Indigenous peoples live in the Arctic. In the 21st century, life in Arctic settlements looks much like life in other parts of the world, despite there being fewer resources. However, Indigenous communities still gather to make political decisions, share resources, and preserve their cultural traditions.

Modern herders

In the past, Indigenous herders used snowshoes, skis, and sleds to drive their reindeer. Today, reindeer herders make use of snowmobiles, helicopters, and even drones to manage their herds across the vast distances of the Arctic.

The covers for the open-top umiak boats are made of bearded seal skin.

Life in Nuuk

Cities in the Arctic, though relatively small, are developed and modern. More than one-third of Greenland's population lives in the island's capital city, Nuuk, which has a combination of colorful wooden houses and modern high-rises.

Snow shelters

Snow houses were traditionally built by some Inuit communities across the Arctic as winter housing. Today, some Inuit hunters still build them as temporary shelters when traveling on land during hunting trips.

High kick

Indigenous athletes across the Arctic compete in traditional sports that test their strength and flexibility. These include the one- or two-foot high kick, in which they leap to kick a hanging ball made of seal skin with one or both feet.

Community festivals

The Iñupiat of Northern Alaska celebrate a summer whaling festival called Nalukataq at which people share local delicacies made of whale meat, blubber, and skin. The highlight of the festival is the blanket toss—the community tosses a person into the air on a blanket made of the animal skins typically used to cover traditional boats.

Food sovereignty

Indigenous Arctic peoples prepare and share the meat of hunted or herded animals using traditional methods. This helps avoid expensive food imports. Here, a Yup'ik woman uses an *ulu* (traditionally, a "woman's knife") to slice salmon for drying.

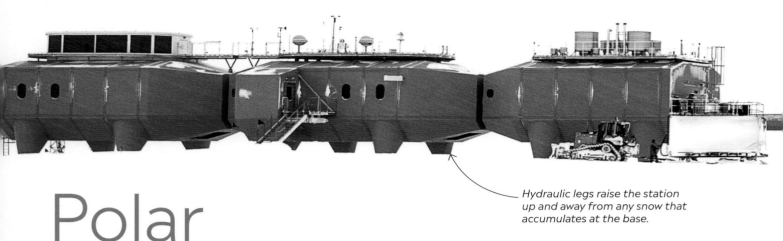

Hydraulic legs raise the station up and away from any snow that accumulates at the base.

Polar
research

Teams of scientists from around the world carry out research at stations in the Arctic and Antarctic. Alongside Indigenous peoples in the Arctic, they study the air, oceans and ice, and life in the polar regions. The information they collect helps scientists understand how these frozen expanses impact the planet, as well as how climate change is affecting them.

Balloons for science

Scientists studying the atmosphere above Antarctica send scientific instruments up in weather balloons to measure temperature, humidity, and atmospheric pressure. Wind speed is measured by tracking the balloon's journey. Once it reaches a high altitude, the balloon bursts, bringing the instruments down. The data collected helps scientists understand environmental changes.

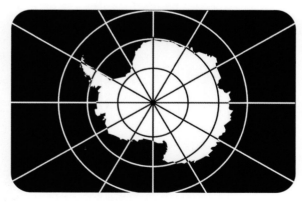

Antarctic cooperation

The 1959 Antarctic Treaty established Antarctica as an international preserve open to scientific research. To date, 56 countries have signed the treaty, which promotes environmental protection, peace, and cooperation between nations.

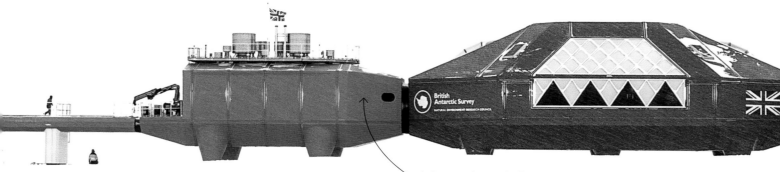

Movable base

The research station Halley VI is on the floating Brunt Ice Shelf in Antarctica. It is the first ever polar station to be built on giant skis so it can be moved, and is constructed with insulated steel to withstand the harsh climate. It houses 16 researchers in winter and up to 70 in summer. If the ice shelf cracks, the station can be dragged along by huge machines to a new location.

Laboratories and offices are housed in blue modules, while a large red module is used for living.

Halley VI is made
up of a string of
8 modules.

Studying the Arctic

The Norwegian town of Ny-Ålesund is the northernmost settlement in the world. Researchers from 11 different countries live and work there. Most of the scientists are trying to understand how the Arctic is changing as it gets steadily warmer. Here, a chemist is taking a sample of Arctic snow for study.

Indigenous knowledge

In the North American Arctic, projects run by communities recognize the traditional knowledge of Indigenous peoples who conduct scientific research in their homelands. The Alaska Arctic Observatory and Knowledge Hub (AAOKH) is a project to share environmental data gathered by Indigenous locals with scientists around the world.

An Indigenous researcher measures the depth of snow in the Arctic.

Arctic Station

The Arctic Station is located on the south coast of Disko Island in Greenland. Researchers here are part of a long-term study to understand the impact of climate change on Arctic ecosystems. They collect data on native animal and plant species, and geological features of the island.

This military transport plane carries researchers from Christchurch, New Zealand, to the ice runway at McMurdo Station in Antarctica.

U.S. AIR FORCE

8199

62ND AW
446TH AW

Life at
polar stations

Life at a polar research station is not easy. All polar researchers are given special training to ensure they can stay safe and cope with the freezing conditions and long, dark winters. Beyond work, the researchers make the most of their unique surroundings and find ways to entertain themselves with activities including musical theater and even dips into icy water.

Dog sleds

While dog sleds are banned on Antarctica, they are still used for traveling in the Arctic. European visitors learned to manage dog sleds from local Indigenous peoples, for whom this is a traditional skill.

Post offices

Before the invention of modern methods of communication, people traveling to polar regions stayed in touch with family through letters. Today, researchers have access to email and social media, but post offices in Antarctica (left) and the Arctic still let them send souvenirs, postcards, and letters.

Getting to the Antarctic

Researchers reach Antarctica from ports in Argentina, Chile, South Africa, New Zealand, and Australia. They take military transport flights, available from a few airports, or find passage on ships. Some countries have modern icebreaker ships that not only carry people to Antarctica, but also conduct research in the region.

Driving over snow

Snowmobiles are the main form of transportation for researchers in Antarctica. These vehicles can pull heavy loads, and can also be roped together to provide safety when traveling over glaciers.

Insulated hooded jacket and ski pants

Protective eyewear

Waterproof outer mitts

Thermal inner mitts

Thermal socks

Padded socks

Staying warm

Surviving icy, windy conditions requires a combination of enough food and warm layers. Humans generate body heat from energy in food, and insulated clothing made with a mix of goose down and weather-resistant fabric traps this heat to keep the researchers warm.

Bottles collect and test seawater temperature and salt levels.

Studying oceans

Polar oceans play an important role in global climate. Researchers on icebreaker ships collect data to understand how these water bodies are changing as Earth gets warmer.

Having fun

When not working, researchers spend their time skiing, snowboarding, or playing other sports. In bad weather, when they stay indoors, they play board games or learn new skills, such as carpentry.

Human impacts on the poles

The Indigenous peoples of the Arctic have lived, hunted, and fished in the far north for thousands of years, maintaining a balance with the environment. However, many nations exploit the natural resources of the polar regions. Now, climate change caused by human activities is melting polar ice and making the oceans more acidic, with devastating results.

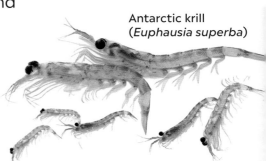

Antarctic krill
(*Euphausia superba*)

Thawing permafrost

The warming of the Arctic is thawing vast stretches of the permafrost (the permanently frozen layer of soil). This causes soil erosion, leading to the collapse of houses and roads. The thawing permafrost also releases large amounts of trapped carbon, further raising global temperatures.

Essential krill

Krill is a small, shrimplike crustacean that is the main source of food for whales, seals, penguins, squids, and seabirds. Krill feed on tiny algae that grow on sea ice. The melting of sea ice due to global warming is affecting krill populations, which will impact the whole food web.

Success story

Humpback whales were once hunted by humans to the brink of extinction. The ban on their commercial hunting is helping this species recover from overexploitation. Numbers have risen to nearly 25,000 individuals. The whale's popularity with tourists and whale-watchers has also helped maintain its populations.

 EYEWITNESS

Sheila Watt-Cloutier
Inuit activist Sheila Watt-Cloutier fights for the rights of the Indigenous peoples of the North American Arctic. She helped achieve a ban on the use of cancer-causing industrial chemicals, which were polluting the Arctic waters and land, and poisoning the animals hunted by the Inuit.

Retreating ice

Melting polar ice—sea ice, ice shelves, and glaciers—has many effects. As the ice melts, it makes the oceans less salty. This affects marine life, and may also affect ocean currents that help keep the climate stable. Melting polar ice adds more water to our seas and oceans, which raises global sea levels over time.

Small sections fall off the Fourcade Glacier in Antarctica.

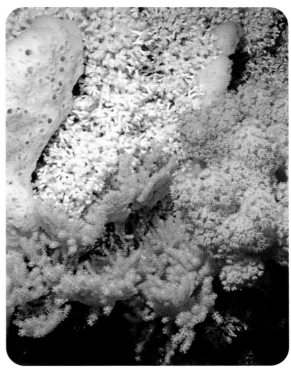

Changing ocean water

As levels of the greenhouse gas carbon dioxide rise in our atmosphere, a lot of it is absorbed by the oceans. This makes the water more acidic, making it difficult for corals and shelled animals to create their external skeletons. Deep-sea corals of the polar regions (above) are most heavily affected by acidic ocean water.

Plastic pollution

Plastics produced by surrounding countries and brought in by wind and ocean currents are a major pollutant in the polar regions. They are found everywhere—on beaches, in snow, and inside many animals. Plastics ingested by animals enter the food chain, including the diet of humans. While researchers are still figuring out their specific, long-term impact, plastics continue to affect life everywhere on our planet.

Mapping
Antarctica

Antarctica is a huge, isolated continent almost entirely covered by ice, where almost no plants can grow. Currents and strong winds sweep around the surrounding oceans, acting as a natural barrier between Antarctica and the rest of the world, and keeping it much colder than the Arctic.

Key to map symbols

- ● Capital city
- ○ Settlement
- ◎ Scientific research station
- △ Mountain
- Glacier
- ⋯⋯ Average limit of summer sea ice, 1981–2010
- ⋯⋯ Average limit of winter sea ice, 1981–2010
- → Warm current
- → Cold current
- ▨ Tundra

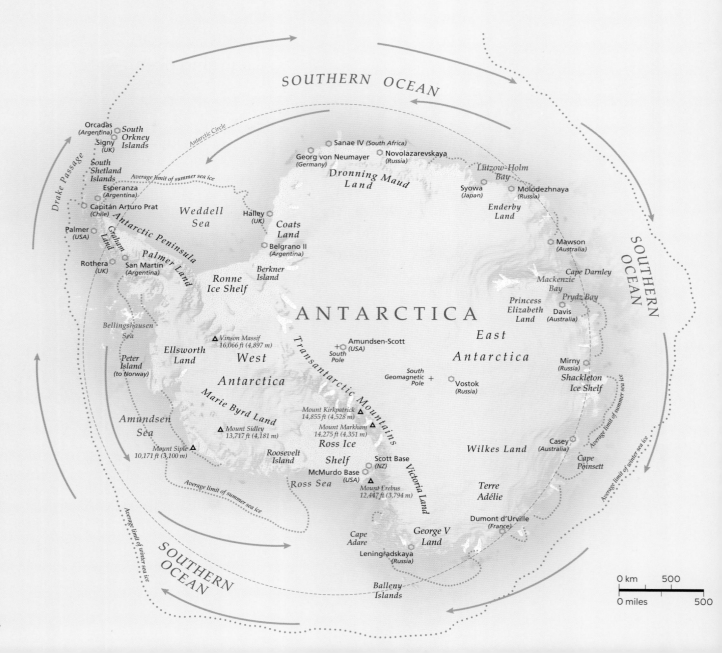

SOUTHERN OCEAN

Orcadas (Argentina)
South Orkney Islands
Signy (UK)

Drake Passage

South Shetland Islands
Esperanza (Argentina)
Capitán Arturo Prat (Chile)
Palmer (USA)
Rothera (UK)
San Martín (Argentina)

Antarctic Circle

Average limit of summer sea ice

Sanae IV (South Africa)
Georg von Neumayer (Germany)
Novolazarevskaya (Russia)

Dronning Maud Land

Lützow-Holm Bay
Syowa (Japan)
Molodezhnaya (Russia)
Enderby Land

Weddell Sea
Halley (UK)
Coats Land
Belgrano II (Argentina)

Antarctic Peninsula
Graham Land
Palmer Land
Ronne Ice Shelf
Berkner Island

Mawson (Australia)
Cape Darnley
Mackenzie Bay
Prydz Bay
Princess Elizabeth Land
Davis (Australia)

ANTARCTICA

East Antarctica

Bellingshausen Sea

Ellsworth Land
Vinson Massif 16,066 ft (4,897 m)
West Antarctica

Amundsen-Scott (USA)
South Pole

Peter Island (to Norway)

Transantarctic Mountains

South Geomagnetic Pole
Vostok (Russia)

Mirny (Russia)
Shackleton Ice Shelf

Marie Byrd Land

Amundsen Sea

Mount Sidley 13,717 ft (4,181 m)
Mount Siple 10,171 ft (3,100 m)

Mount Kirkpatrick 14,855 ft (4,528 m)
Mount Markham 14,275 ft (4,351 m)

Ross Ice Shelf

Roosevelt Island

Wilkes Land
Casey (Australia)
Cape Poinsett

Scott Base (NZ)

McMurdo Base (USA)

Ross Sea
Mount Erebus 12,447 ft (3,794 m)

Victoria Land
Terre Adélie

Average limit of summer sea ice

Cape Adare

George V Land
Leningradskaya (Russia)

Dumont d'Urville (France)

SOUTHERN OCEAN

Average limit of winter sea ice

Balleny Islands

SOUTHERN OCEAN

Average limit of summer sea ice

Average limit of winter sea ice

0 km		500
0 miles		500

Mapping the **Arctic**

The Arctic is less isolated than the Antarctic, since the northern continents extend well inside the Arctic Circle. Much of the deep Arctic Ocean is covered by permanent pack ice. The biggest area of land ice is the Greenland Ice Sheet.

EXTREME SEASONS

Earth spins at an angle. The North and South poles experience extreme seasons when they are tilted toward or away from the sun. This diagram shows how the Antarctic receives 24 hours of daylight during the southern midsummer (December 21 or 22), while the Arctic lies in winter darkness.

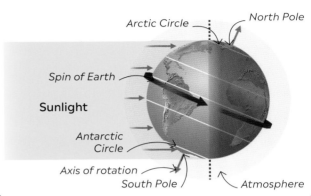

Arctic Circle — *North Pole*
Spin of Earth
Sunlight
Antarctic Circle
Axis of rotation — *South Pole* — *Atmosphere*

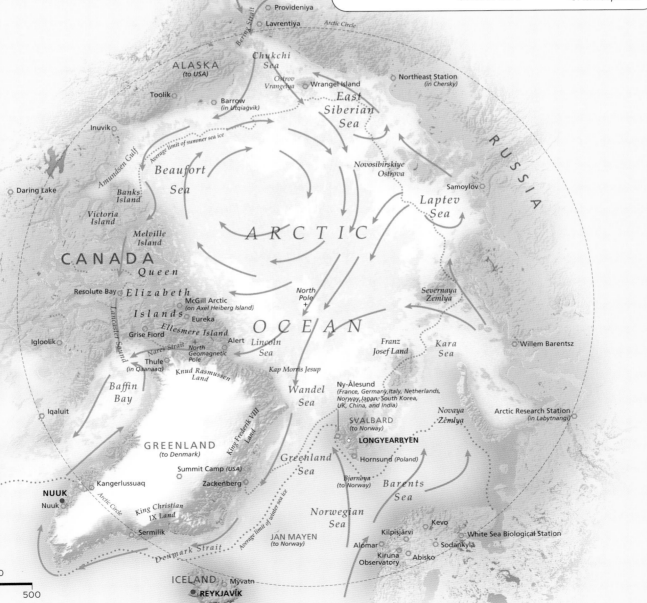

Provideniya
Lavrentiya
Arctic Circle
Chukchi Sea
ALASKA (to USA)
Ostrov Vrangelya — Wrangel Island
Northeast Station (in Chersky)
Toolik
Barrow (in Utqiagvik)
East Siberian Sea
Inuvik
RUSSIA
Average limit of summer sea ice
Beaufort Sea
Novosibirskiye Ostrova
Samoylov
Daring Lake
Amundsen Gulf
Banks Island
Laptev Sea
Victoria Island
A R C T I C
Melville Island
CANADA
Queen
Severnaya Zemlya
Resolute Bay
Elizabeth
McGill Arctic (on Axel Heiberg Island)
North Pole +
Igloolik
Islands
Eureka
Ellesmere Island
Grise Fiord
O C E A N
Franz Josef Land
Kara Sea
Willem Barentsz
Nares Strait
Alert
Lincoln Sea
Thule (in Qaanaaq)
+ North Geomagnetic Pole
Kap Morris Jesup
Knud Rasmussen Land
Baffin Bay
Wandel Sea
Ny-Ålesund (France, Germany, Italy, Netherlands, Norway, Japan, South Korea, UK, China, and India)
Novaya Zemlya
Arctic Research Station (in Labytnangi)
Iqaluit
SVALBARD (to Norway)
LONGYEARBYEN
King Frederik VIII Land
GREENLAND (to Denmark)
Hornsund (Poland)
Summit Camp (USA)
Zackenberg
Greenland Sea
Bjørnøya (to Norway)
Barents Sea
NUUK
Nuuk
Kangerlussuaq
Arctic Circle
King Christian IX Land
Norwegian Sea
Kevo
Sermilik
Average limit of winter sea ice
JAN MAYEN (to Norway)
Kilpisjärvi
White Sea Biological Station
Denmark Strait
Alomar
Sodankyla
Kiruna Observatory
Abisko
0 km 250 500
0 miles 250 500
ICELAND — Mývatn
REYKJAVÍK

Polar climate

Ever since Earth formed, polar climates have been changing—20 million years ago, there was no ice in the polar regions, but 20,000 years ago, Earth was in the grip of an ice age. We are now in a period of rapid warming. The effects could be dramatic, on both the polar regions and the rest of the world.

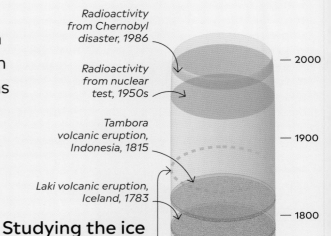

Radioactivity from Chernobyl disaster, 1986

Radioactivity from nuclear test, 1950s

Tambora volcanic eruption, Indonesia, 1815

Laki volcanic eruption, Iceland, 1783

— 2000

— 1900

— 1800

Studying the ice
This illustration of an ice core (ice cylinder drilled from an ice sheet) from the Greenland Ice Sheet tells us a lot about the last 1,000 years. It is made of compressed snow built in layers over time. Tiny air bubbles trapped in it tell us about the levels of specific gases in the atmosphere at different points in history. The ice also tells us about temperature changes through time.

— 1700

— 1600

Annual mean summer temperature in Arctic 32°F (0°C)

Annual mean summer temperature in Antarctic -18.4°F (-28°C)

Annual mean winter temperature in Arctic -40°F (-40°C)

Coldest point in Arctic (Klinck Station, Greenland) -93.3°F (-69.6°C)

20°C
0°C
-20°C
-60°C
-80°C
-100°C

50°F
10°F
-18.4°F
-70°F
-110°F
-150°F

Annual mean winter temperature in Antarctic -76°F (-60°C)

Coldest point in Antarctic (Vostok Station) -128°F (-89°C)

Little ice age— a series of cold periods in the northern hemisphere, 1450-1850

— 1500

Öraefajökull volcanic eruption, Iceland, 1362

— 1400

How cold?
Antarctica is much colder than the Arctic because it is a deep-frozen continent, while the Arctic is mostly ocean that is frozen only at the surface.

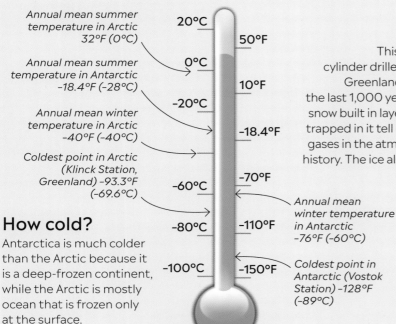

Carbon dioxide in the atmosphere
(from the Vostok ice core)

Carbon dioxide
The Vostok ice core (an ice core taken from the center of the ice sheet in Vostok, Russia) shows how carbon dioxide (CO_2) levels have fluctuated over the past 400,000 years. Air samples since 1950 show much higher levels of this gas.

— 1300

— 1200

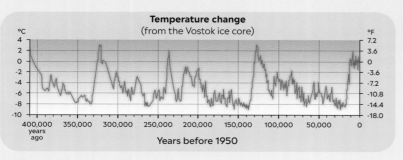

Temperature change
(from the Vostok ice core)

Temperature
Fluctuations in the local air temperature match the changes in CO_2 recorded in the same period. Since CO_2 in the air helps keep Earth warm, higher levels of this gas lead to higher temperatures.

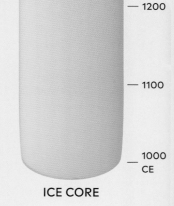

ICE CORE

— 1100

— 1000
CE

GREENHOUSE EFFECTS

• Earth's atmosphere acts as insulation that stops heat escaping into space. Without it, the average global temperature would be 54°F (30°C) lower, the oceans would freeze, and life would be impossible. The insulation is called the greenhouse effect.
• It is caused by certain gases in the atmosphere that absorb heat radiated by the planet. These include carbon dioxide (CO_2), methane, and nitrous oxide.
• If more CO_2 or other greenhouse gases are added to the atmosphere, it retains more heat. This raises global temperatures.
• The extra CO_2 in the air is mainly released by burning coal, oil, and natural gas to fuel transportation and generate electricity. The more fuel we burn, the more CO_2 is released, causing our climate to change.

Larsen B, January 2002

Shrinking sea ice

The rise in global temperatures has caused polar sea ice—ice that floats on polar oceans—to slowly melt. While the cover of Arctic sea ice has been shrinking for decades, until recently the sea ice around Antarctica was growing. But in 2016 scientists noticed that Antarctica's sea ice had begun shrinking annually, as seen in the chart below.

Antarctic annual minimum sea ice extent
1979–2023

[Line chart showing Extent (million square kilometers) on y-axis from 0.0 to 4.0, and Year on x-axis from 1978 to 2023. Values fluctuate between roughly 2.0 and 3.75, with a dotted expected average line dropping toward 1.5 at the end.]

◆ Average for each year   ⋯⋯ Expected average for 2023–2024 and beyond

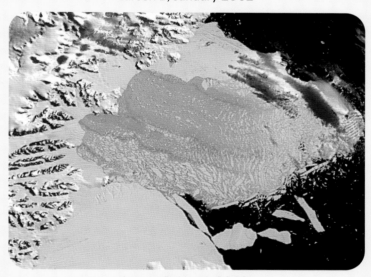

Larsen B, March 2002

Ice shelf collapse

Ice shelves support the edges of Antarctica, but they are collapsing due to rising temperatures. The Antarctic Peninsula was bordered by a floating ice shelf divided into three parts—Larsen A, B, and C. Larsen A broke up in 1995. Larsen B collapsed dramatically in 2002, forming pools of meltwater and thousands of icebergs (above). Larsen C lost a large section in 2017.

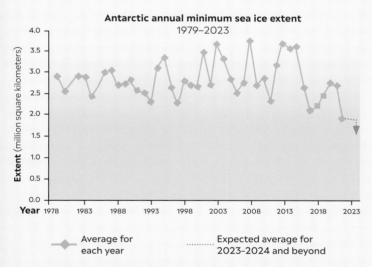

Rising sea levels

The melting polar ice sheets are pouring vast amounts of meltwater into the warming oceans, which is raising sea levels. This is a serious problem for people living on low-lying coral islands, such as the Maldives in the Indian Ocean. Waves surging farther inland at high tide swamp coastal houses on these islands and contaminate water supplies. No one knows exactly when and how the polar ice sheets will melt. But, if they collapse suddenly far more ice will slip into the sea, and coastal cities could be under threat.

Species status

Polar animals face many challenges. Global warming is melting the sea ice that many animals depend on for shelter and hunting. They also face food shortages because of overfishing by humans, or can get entangled in fishing gear themselves.

BLACK-BROWED ALBATROSS

Thalassarche melanophris

Location: Breeding on subantarctic islands around the Southern Ocean

Numbers are declining for this relatively common albatross, which often gets entangled in fishing gear and dies. At present, there are an estimated 600,000 breeding pairs.

ARCTIC FOX

Vulpes lagopus

Location: Tundra regions

Although protected in Scandinavia, where numbers are low, this animal is widespread in the rest of the Arctic and not considered threatened.

EMPEROR PENGUIN

Aptenodytes forsteri

Location: Antarctica, breeding on sea ice

There are around 270,000 breeding pairs on Antarctic ice shelves. However, rapidly melting sea ice is making it a challenge for them to find places to breed and raise their chicks.

WALRUS

Odobenus rosmarus

Location: Arctic Ocean, migrating to subarctic areas in winter

Walruses are vulnerable due to declining sea ice, which they use for resting and giving birth.

POLAR BEAR

Ursus maritimus

Location: Coasts and frozen seas of the Arctic and subarctic

Reduced sea ice, where polar bears do their hunting, is likely to drastically affect their numbers, estimated at 22,000 to 31,000 at present.

BOWHEAD WHALE

Balaena mysticetus

Location: Arctic Ocean, migrating to subarctic seas in winter

This is the only large whale to stay in northern waters all year round. It was once heavily hunted by commercial whalers for oil and baleen. It is now sustainably hunted by Inuit and Yupiit communities.

LEOPARD SEAL

Hydrurga leptonyx

Location: Antarctica and subantarctic islands

This aggressive predator is not thought to be under threat at present. Estimates of its total population range to more than 400,000 individuals.

ARCTIC WOLF

Canis lupus arctos

Location: Tundra of Canadian Arctic islands and Greenland

This subspecies of the gray wolf is found in remote regions, where it hunts the musk ox and other prey. It is not considered to be under threat.

SNOWY OWL

Bubo scandiacus

Location: Arctic tundra, sometimes flying south in winter

These versatile predators hunt both by day and at night. Their numbers seem to be decreasing due to the warming climate.

BELUGA WHALE

Delphinapterus leucas

Location: Arctic and north temperate waters, often among sea ice

Some southerly populations of this widespread species have declined, especially those in Canada's St. Lawrence Estuary. Pollution is affecting their health.

WOLVERINE

Gulo gulo

Location: North America and Eurasia, from Arctic to temperate regions

Wolverines were once trapped extensively for their fur. They now survive at low densities across northern forests, mountains, and tundra lands.

MUSK OX

Ovibos moschatus

Location: Tundra of northern Canada and Greenland

Musk oxen are flourishing. They have also been reintroduced to Alaska and northern Eurasia, where they last lived thousands of years ago.

Glossary

ADAPTATION A feature of a living thing that helps it thrive in its environment and lifestyle. Adaptations are passed on to offspring and evolve over generations.

ANTARCTIC CIRCLE An imaginary line around the south polar region of Earth. South of the circle, there is at least one day of 24-hour daylight and one day of 24-hour darkness per year.

ANTARCTIC PENINSULA A point of land that stretches northward toward South America on Antarctica's west side, with milder habitats than the rest of Antarctica.

ARCTIC CIRCLE An imaginary line around the north polar region. North of the line, there is at least one day of 24-hour daylight and one day of 24-hour darkness per year.

AURORA Also known as the northern and southern lights, flickering lights in the night sky sometimes visible in the lower polar regions, caused by the interaction between high-energy particles from the sun and Earth's magnetic field.

BIVALVE An aquatic, invertebrate animal that has two shells of equal size connected by a flexible ligament, which allows it to open and close around the animal. They are found in marine, fresh, and brackish water. Examples include clams, oysters, mussels, and scallops.

BLUBBER Fat that forms an insulating layer under the skin of whales, seals, and many seabirds.

CARNIVORE A meat-eating animal; specifically, a member of the order Carnivora, the mammal group that includes dogs, cats, bears, and seals.

CLIMATE CHANGE Changing global weather patterns over long periods of time. Greenhouse gas emissions from human activities, such as coal burning, are a leading cause of climate change.

Aurora australis (southern lights) at Amundsen–Scott South Pole Station

CORALS Simple marine animals related to sea anemones. They grow in colonies fixed to a particular spot, supported by a skeleton, and grab their food from the passing water.

CRUSTACEANS Invertebrate animals with jointed limbs and a hard outer skeleton.

ENDANGERED A species of plant or animal considered at risk of extinction in the wild, either due to a decrease of its population or a loss of its habitat.

FROSTBITE An injury to the skin and underlying body tissues, caused by exposure to extreme cold.

GLACIER A mass of land ice slowly flowing downhill.

GLOBAL WARMING The current warming trend in Earth's atmosphere and oceans, thought to be due to increases in greenhouse gases.

GREENHOUSE GAS Any gas in the atmosphere that tends to absorb heat radiating from Earth's surface, causing the atmosphere to warm up.

ICE AGE One of a series of prolonged periods of extreme cold alternating with milder spells over the last 2.5 million years, when thick ice sheets covered much of Earth's surface; more specifically, the most recent cold spell ending around 10,000 years ago.

ICEBERG A large mass of freshwater ice that has broken off ("calved") from a glacier or ice shelf and floats in the sea.

ICE CAP A mass of permanent land ice similar to an ice sheet but smaller in extent.

ICE FLOE A drifting section of broken-up sea ice.

Icebergs in Jökulsárlón glacier lagoon, Iceland

ICE SHEET A very large mass of permanent ice covering land.

ICE SHELF An ice mass extending out to sea but attached to land and which begins as ice flowing from an ice sheet. It can be 330–3,280 ft (100–1,000 m) thick in places. The largest ice shelves in the world are found in Antarctica.

INVERTEBRATE Any animal without a backbone, including worms, snails, shrimp, starfish, and coral.

KRILL Shrimplike animals that swim and feed in huge numbers as part of the plankton of polar seas, and in turn are food for many larger animals.

LICHEN A unique living organism that is a partnership between a fungus and a simple plant (an alga). Small and hardy, lichens can grow as crusts on dry rocks or in leafy or bushy forms.

MAMMAL A warm-blooded animal, such as a human, dog, cat, seal, deer, or whale, that suckles its young.

MIGRATION A regular (usually yearly) large-scale movement of animals of a particular species from one region to another and back again.

MOLLUSKS A major group of invertebrate animals that includes snails, slugs, clams, octopuses, and squid, which share the same basic body plan despite their different shapes.

MOSS A simple low-growing green plant that is nonflowering and lacks stems and roots.

NORTH POLE The location at which Earth's axis (the imaginary line around which Earth spins) reaches the surface of the Arctic Ocean.

OZONE LAYER A region high in Earth's atmosphere containing the gas ozone (a form of oxygen) that protects life on Earth from harmful ultraviolet radiation.

PACK ICE Drifting sea ice, especially when it has been broken up by wave action and then frozen together again.

PERMAFROST Frozen ground found beneath the surface in polar regions. Ground frozen for two or more years continuously can be called permafrost, but some permafrost is thousands of years old.

PLANKTON Plants or animals living in open water that cannot swim strongly and so drift with the currents. They are usually small or microscopic.

SCAVENGER An animal that feeds on dead or decaying animals, or on the remains of hunted animals.

SCIENTIFIC NAME The official name of a species, normally printed in *italic* type. It consists of two words: a genus name written with a capital letter, and a species name without one. For example, *Ursus maritimus* is the scientific name of the polar bear.

SEA ICE Ice that has formed directly on the sea, in contrast to land-formed ice such as an ice shelf or iceberg. It is usually less than 16 ft (5 m) thick.

SEA URCHIN A rounded, spiny, non-swimming animal related to starfish.

SHELLFISH Marine invertebrates that have hard outer shells, especially mollusks and crustaceans.

SOUTH POLE The point at which Earth's axis (the imaginary line around which Earth spins), reaches the surface of the Antarctic continent.

SOUTHERN OCEAN The ocean surrounding Antarctica, formed by the southernmost parts of the Pacific, Atlantic, and Indian oceans.

SQUID Fast-swimming marine invertebrates of the open ocean related to octopuses, with two long tentacles and eight shorter arms.

SUBANTARCTIC Regions north of Antarctica where weather conditions are less severe than in Antarctica itself. The phrase "subantarctic islands" refers to any of the numerous islands dotting the ocean north of Antarctica.

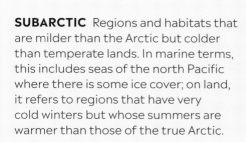

Flock of snow geese in flight during migration

SUBARCTIC Regions and habitats that are milder than the Arctic but colder than temperate lands. In marine terms, this includes seas of the north Pacific where there is some ice cover; on land, it refers to regions that have very cold winters but whose summers are warmer than those of the true Arctic.

TEMPERATE Regions between the tropics and the polar regions that have moderate temperatures.

TRANSANTARCTIC MOUNTAINS The longest mountain range in Antarctica, dividing the continent into East and West Antarctica.

TUNDRA A flat landscape that is dominated by low-growing, cold-tolerant plants. Tundra is widespread in northern North America and Eurasia.

ULTRAVIOLET Invisible high-energy light radiated from the sun that can sometimes damage living things. Much of it is absorbed by Earth's ozone layer.

Tundra landscape in Denali National Park, Alaska

Index

Acknowledgments

The publisher would like to thank the following people for their help with making the book:
Carron Brown, Vandana Likhmania, and Nandana Saikia for editorial assistance; Ivan Finnegan, Kati Poynor, Robin Hunter, Manisha Patel, Andrew Nash, Susan St. Louis, and Aude van Ryn for design and illustration assistance; Hazel Beynon for proofreading; Elizabeth Wise for the index; Open Air Cambridge Ltd. for the use of their clothing and equipment; the staff of Tierpark Dählhölzli, Bern, Switzerland, for their time and trouble; Tony Hall at the Royal Botanical Gardens, Kew; Julia Nicholson and the staff of the Pitt Rivers Museum, Oxford; Robert Headland and the staff of the Scott Polar Research Institute, Cambridge; Whipsnade Zoo, Bedfordshire; and The British School of Falconry, Gleneagles, Scotland.

Additional photography: Harry Taylor at the Natural History Museum (45tl); University Museum, Cambridge (43cr); Jerry Young (32/33, 40tl). **Maps:** Simon Mumford; Sallie Alane Reason. **Model:** Gordon Models

The publisher would like to thank the following for their kind permission to reproduce their images:

(a=above; b=below/bottom; c=center; f=far; l=left; r=right; t=top)

123RF.com: pilipenkod 15tl; /sandermeertinsphotography 24–25c; /alancotton 58clb. **Aardman Animations:** 36cr; /Jean-Paul Ferrero 28tr. **Alamy Stock Photo:** Colin Harris / era-images 4crb, 10tr; /Top-Pics TBK 4cra, 49cr; /MET / BOT 4br, 51cra; /blickwinkel 6–7ca; /imageBROKER.com GmbH & Co. KG 7tr, 47cra, 60cra; /Zoonar GmbH 9crb, 40cl; /All Canada Photos 10c; /Eric Carr 10–11b; /Minden Pictures 12crb, 13tr, 21cr, 32bl, 41cra, 45r; /Arto Hakola 14cl, 38–39b; /Avalon. red 14–15ca; /Nature Picture Library 16tr, 39tr, 44cra; /

Imagebroker 16–17b; /elementix 17crb; /Martin Hughes-Jones 19l; /Kevin Murch 19tc; /Ralph Lee Hopkins 19bc; /Minkimo 20tl; /robertharding 22–23t, 46–47c, 60bl; /Steven J. Kazlowski 23clb, 57tl, 59bl; /Paul Couvrette 25tc; /The Granger Collection 26cra; /David Tipling Photo Library 27r; /Diana Rebman 29tc; /Stuart Holroyd 30–31t, 58–59t; /Michael Cummings 34tl; /Phil Degginger 36tl; wesdotphotography 36bl; /Stock Connection Blue 38tr; /FLPA 40bl; /blickwinkel 41l; /Louise Murray 45cl; /Roberto Cornacchia 48–49t; /Danita Delimont 50cr; /The Canadian Press / Christopher Katsarov 51ca; /PA Images 55tr; /Emma Wood 56t; /Sren Andersson / TT News Agency / kod 1037 57br; /Martin Nielsen 59crb; /Cavan Images 60–61t; /Sabena Jane Blackbird 61cb; /AP Photo / Chris Windeyer, The Canadian Press 62br; /Sergi Reboredo 62clb; /Ashley Cooper pics 63crb; /Mint Images Limited 63l; /Science History Images 67tr. **B. & C. Alexander:** 6/7b, 11ctr, 25br, 39tl, 44bl; /British Library 7tl; /National Maritime Museum 52bl. **Bruce Coleman Ltd.:** 35bl, 37tl; /Keith Nels Swenson 11ctl. **Caters Media Group:** 29cra. **Corbis:** Michael S. Nolan / Terra 6–7b. **Dorling Kindersley:** Pitt Rivers Museum, University of Oxford 2bc, 48bc; /Jerry Young 4clb. **Dreamstime.com:** Anna Kucherova 1c; /Alexey Sedov 8bl, 17tr; /Svetlana Foote 20cl; /Galinasavina 33tl; /Yuriy Barbaruk 35cl; /Jim Cumming 40cr; /Slowmotiongli 47bl; /Vadim Nefedov 56bl; /Gentoomultimedia 68c. **Frank Lane Picture Agency:** Hannu Hautala 17tcl; /Peter Moore 15cr; /F. Pölking 32cl; /Mark Newman 38c; /Tony Wharton 17tl. **Getty Images:** Tom Brakefield / Photodisc 71tr; Yvette Cardozo / Workbook Stock 69c; /Daniel J. Cox / Photographer's Choice 69bl; Peter Lilja / The Image Bank 68tr; Nathalie Michel / The Image Bank 69tl; Enrique Aguirre Aves / Photodisc 2br, 28bc; /Daniel Parent 5tr; /De Agostini Picture Library 6tr; /Pierre Longnus / The Image Bank 19cr; /Tim P. Whitby / Getty Images for the Natural History Museum 28clb; /MB Photography / Moment 28cla; /Auscape / Universal Images Group 31crb; /Kim Heacox 42clb; /Michael Robinson

Chavez / The Washington Post 62cl; /Westend61 67bl. **Getty Images / iStock:** KeithSzafranski / E+ 30crb; /Anagramm 69br. **L. David Mech:** 41br. **Mark Mallory:** 21cra. **Mary Evans Picture Library:** 9tr, 42tl, 54bl, 55bc. **Courtesy of the National Science Foundation:** Rhys Boulton 70cl. **Natural History Photographic Agency:** Melvin Grey 20/21b; /Brian Hawkes 29tl; /E.A. James 29tr; /Peter Johnson 27c; /Stephen Krasemann 37tr; /Lady Philippa Scott 27bl. **naturepl.com:** Pascal Kobeh 2clb, 12c; /Franco Banfi 12bl, 13br; /Doug Allan 12–13tc; /Alex Mustard 21crb; /Solvin Zankl 27cla; /Konrad Wothe 42cla; /Heike Odermatt 42–43bc; /Doug Allan 44cl; /Brian Skerry 46tr; /Frederique Olivier 61cra; /Florian Graner 63tr. **Norwegian Institute for Nature Research – NINA:** Roy Andersen 39cr. **Ocean Alliance whale.org:** 46br. **Oxford Scientific Films:** Colin Monteath 22b. **Patrick J. Endres / Alaskaphotographics.com:** 56–57c. **Reuters:** Lisi Niesner 59cl. **Robert Harding Picture Library:** Michael Nolan 6–7b; / Ingrid Visser 29b. **Roger Key:** 18cb. **Royal Geographical Society:** 53cr, 53tr; /Alastair Laidlaw 53br. **Science Photo Library:** British Antarctic Survey 4cla, 10cl, 10bl, 58cr; / Martin Camm / Carwardine 47cra. **Shutterstock.com:** Michele Aldeghi 14–15b; /Tarpan 23bc; / Agami Photo Agency 26bl; /polarman 61br. **Simon Morley:** Stephanie Martin 13bc. **SuperStock:** Alaska Stock 57bl.

All other images © Dorling Kindersley Limited

Every effort has been made to trace the copyright holders. Dorling Kindersley apologizes for any unintentional omissions and would be pleased, in such cases, to add an acknowledgment in future editions.